From

The \
124 Shoredit

80p

Healthy Planet
Books for Free

You've rescued me from going to waste

- healthyplanet.org
- healthy_planet
- healthyplanet

Grace Bartram

Grace Bartram has been for many years a freelance writer and photojournalist for newspapers and radio in Australia and New Zealand. She has worked for four years in a women's refuge and is currently involved in a women's resource centre in New South Wales, with the Women's Electoral Lobby and the peace movement.

Since her children grew up, she has devoted herself increasingly to fiction, and has had two volumes published in Australia.

GRACE BARTRAM

Peeling

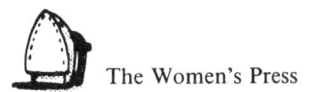

The Women's Press

First published by The Women's Press Limited 1986
A member of the Namara Group
124 Shoreditch High Street, London E1 6JE

Copyright © Grace Bartram 1986

All rights reserved. This book is a work of fiction and any resemblance to persons living or dead is purely coincidental.

British Library Cataloguing in Publication Data

Bartram, Grace
  Peeling
  I. Title
  823[F]   PR9619.3.B/

  ISBN 0-7043-2878-X
  ISBN 0-7043-3994-3 Pbk

One

Rowley was standing at the window, deep-breathing, fingers intertwined behind neat bottom, his head sinking to knee level as he expelled the air from his lungs.

Ally watched her husband sleepily.

'Rowley, do you have to go to the office this morning or can we go for a walk?'

Rowley had stopped exercising, and belatedly she realised he was pulling on shorts and a cotton shirt.

'I'm not going to the city dressed like this, Ally, am I?'

He sat down and reached for his sneakers.

His eyes were light blue, very attractive in such a tanned face. His hair was greying at the sides, enhancing an air of distinction. He was a little over six feet and weighed a trim eleven stone.

When he spoke again, she was surprised to note there was strain in his voice.

'I'm going to make a cup of tea, then we'll walk. I want to talk to you.'

'I'll have a shower.'

She jumped out of bed.

Ally and Rowley were the same age, but it seemed to her that, at fifty-four, Rowley looked youthful, distinguished and full of vitality, while she felt herself to be some kind of vanishing woman. People seemed to look past her, rather than at her. Shop assistants tended to give her bored, glazed looks and a sharp 'What?', so that often she had to repeat what she'd asked for.

Smoothing soapsuds over her face, she thought that men could grow moustaches and beards to hide deepening lines and wrinkles, while post-menopausal women peered every morning into magnifying mirrors, plucking hairs from the upper lip and around the chin. Ally giggled. How'd it be if you let the hairs grow and incorporate themselves into a wispy moustache? Her daughter, Jane, had once told her about a woman in a female rock band, who'd cultivated a miniature van Dyck beard from a few straggling chin hairs.

At the thought of Jane, Ally felt a nagging unease. She looked down at her legs, decided they could wait until tomorrow for a shave.

Out of the shower, she glimpsed herself in the steamed-up mirror, wiped the surface with the edge of her towel, looked at herself closely. Not bad, but not as good as Rowley; still slim, but parts of her starting to sag. She swivelled and looked at her buttocks. Were they beginning to droop? She tightened the muscles. No, not really; her bum was still quite taut. She heard cups rattling in the kitchen, put on a cotton housecoat, zipped it up and went out.

In this house overlooking the ocean, Ally was often alone. Rowley maintained a large flat close to the city. At some point in the past few years it had become his principal residence. They weren't separated, had never even thought of such a thing; it was just that he loved city life and she loved the beach house.

Ally took the tea he handed her.

'I've been thinking, it'd be nice to drive up together and see Jane. Could you get away some time soon?'

Rowley had his back to her, examining one of his paintings, to her eyes a confusion of brightly-hued dots and slashes; a waste of money, she thought.

'Ally, I realise you miss Jane but I don't think she'd appreciate a visit from us. She's nearly twenty-eight, you know, and she wants to live her own life, no matter what we think of it.'

'Oh, Rowley, I *know* all that. I worry about her, I can't help it. I never did like Marjorie, from the first time she came here. What are they doing up there in that valley? I wish Marjorie would leave Jane alone.'

'Just be thankful Jane's not into drugs.'

'How do you know she isn't? Maybe that's why she's gone away.'

'I know her better than that.'

'I hope you're right.'

'I know I'm right.'

Ally put her cup down and tea splashed on the cloth, soaking the white and gold daisy pattern. She jumped up quickly and removed the cloth from the table, going to the sink to run water over it before the stain set. Then later, as she ran down the long hallway in shorts and shirt, she bumped into a tall vase Rowley had imported from Italy, causing it to spin half a revolution before settling down again.

Ally stared nervously at it as though it had become animate. It might well have been, the way it had terrorised her from the moment Rowley had placed it there, ignoring her protest that it would get broken.

When she came out on to the wide veranda, her husband was walking through the trees below. A low swell creamed the beach, points of light winking and flashing over the vast expanse of water.

How she loved this small, old house by the ocean. Rowley tolerated it at weekends, remote from all his interests. He'd made a great deal of money importing beautiful and elegant things. To Ally's discomfort, their homes had always been graced with exquisite objects and fine furniture, position ordained by Rowley. She'd always been fearful of breaking, scratching, mistreating, failing to give proper care and maintenance. A certain, secret slothfulness constantly threatened.

The things she collected had been made beautiful by natural forces, grinding of sand and water, bleaching of sun's rays; driftwood, rolled stones, shells, glass balls netted with rope, smelling of tar and fish and salt; fragments of smooth-worn glass, once an ancient bottle crusted with delicate coral like stiffened lace.

Of all those things once found and cherished, only stones and driftwood remained. Fishermen used float balls made of plastic, shells seemed to have vanished, ugly plastic containers rode to shore and once nested on the sand grew uglier with time. Ally hurried after Rowley. She was always dawdling behind people. As a child she'd given her mother endless trouble when going to school, often having to be dragged to the end of the street and set on her way with a whack on the bottom.

Once her mother had turned away, Ally would climb through a gap in a fence, slide down a wet, grassy bank to a dank canal, beside which was a narrow path. She'd run, soothing herself with the hypnotic rhythm that developed as she jumped from side to side on the bluestone blocks which lined the canal.

She'd never forgotten the smell of it, a metallic, damp odour, like an old spoon encrusted with verdigris. Sometimes the canal ran with water so savagely piled, that she'd have drowned if she'd fallen in. She'd edge her way along, gazing dizzily at the way it crested and whirlpooled.

At the thought of flood waters she shivered and reflected on how terrified her parents would have been had they known how the canal drew her. And when she'd reached the bridge where she could pull herself up a bank made slippery with onion weed, through a white fence with peeling paint, she'd look anxiously towards the school, knowing she was late again.

She'd sneak through the forbidden territory of the high-ceilinged entrance hall, tiptoeing its polished parquet floor, hiding behind a door from which she could slip out unobserved and join the other children as they trooped up to the classrooms after assembly in the quadrangle.

How it had dominated her life and how miserable she'd been all through schooldays.

Rowley had turned and was jogging towards her. Something on his mind, she knew by his impatience. Perhaps it was business. Perhaps they had to economise, sell the beach house, live in the city. Not that, she couldn't stand that. Better if he retired and lived at the beach with her. The beach house had always been more hers than Rowley's. At first they went to it only for holidays, then, when Jane left school, they'd sold the suburban house and moved to the flat. Ally had hated it. She began spending more and more time at the beach until, without any discussion she could recall, it had become accepted as Ally's place.

She stopped and stared at the sand. How very strange that they'd never talked about it. Rowley jogged past without looking at her. She'd noticed that joggers never spoke to anyone, or smiled or said 'Hi' as they passed. Jane said it disturbed their concentration.

Ally kept walking towards the headland, climbed the steep track and waited at the top. If they had to talk, she'd choose a territory that was hers, up there where the wind blew and the horizon retreated. The growth on the headland followed its shape, low, scrubby trees moulded over hard ground, like rough fur on a lean animal.

If it was business, maybe she could help. Before the birth of Jane she'd enjoyed going to the office, though, come to think of it, Rowley had never encouraged her. Once she had Jane it was easier to stay away, except for an occasional selfconscious visit when shopping in the city.

Rowley wasn't a man who enjoyed sharing things with a wife, or maybe she hadn't been the right kind of wife for him to enjoy sharing things with.

He played the stock market. Jane said he was considered brilliant at it. She said Ally should have taken more interest in business and finance, scorning women who were mere wives and mothers, while Ally thought her role was to provide husband and daughter with a comfortable and tranquil home.

Rowley appeared at the top of the track.

'You look hot. Come and sit down.'

He did, but not close to her.

'Is it business that's on your mind, Rowley? I'm not surprised. I always thought inflation was when your dollar buys less and that's still happening, so how come they keep saying it's under control when every housewife knows it isn't?'

Rowley was too out of breath to speak.

'Nothing ever comes down in price,' Ally went on. 'Isn't that inflation, when things keep rising all the time?'

Rowley still hadn't recovered his wind after the jog and the climb. Between gasps he said: 'I didn't come up here to respond to one of your homilies on the economy, Ally, and there's nothing wrong with my business.'

Immediately, the spectre of cancer entered her mind, though Rowley had stopped smoking years earlier. He'd had a medical check-up during the week.

'Did the doctor find something?'

'I'm in perfect health, Ally, never better. Would you just keep quiet and let me talk?'

He stood and walked around. Ally folded her arms. He came back and looked down at her.

'Ally, we've had some good years.'

'Yes, we've had good times,' – searching her memory fruitlessly for some really good times they'd had, feeling bleak when none surfaced.

'I've looked after you financially and I always will.'

'I never worry about money.'

'Ally, our marriage isn't what it was when we started out, you realise that?'

Ally's heart speeded up its beat.

'Rowley, what are you trying to say?'

He cleared his throat, said: 'Ally, people, well, people no longer expect to have only one marriage, stay with one person all their lives. It's unrealistic to imagine you can share the same interests for fifty years. It's ridiculous. People grow. In different ways, different directions.'

She stood up, not wanting to sit like a dummy while he made up new rules. Rowley got so damned pompous sometimes.

'I expect people to stay together. I expect to stay with you, Rowley.'

She looked up at the sky, the great, blue sweep of it.

'I haven't changed. We do have interests, friends, don't we? Fleur, and, well, we both know Fleur and she was my *bridesmaid*, that's how long we've known her. I feel the same about you as I did then.'

A detached, inner voice was more objective, saying, you don't feel the same about him, not really.

'Ally, I suppose I'm talking about *not* changing, that's really what I'm getting at. You haven't changed. I'm the one who's changed. Goddammit, Ally, why do I always get confused when I have a discussion with you? Look, all your interests are here at the beach. You never come to the flat any more. You're not interested in my business or anything else I do.'

'Well, that's not fair. You discouraged me. If that's what you're on about I don't mind changing. I'd like to know more about the business.'

'Ally, I don't want to hurt you. How can I explain it to you? Look, you still wear the same colour lipstick, you haven't changed it since I first met you . . .'

She stared at him, astonished.

'Haven't you noticed, women wear different lipstick now, if they wear any at all, yet you wear a brand and a colour that hasn't altered in thirty years.'

'Are you crazy, Rowley? What's lipstick got to do with a lasting marriage?'

'You still do your hair the same way, you still read the damned *Women's Weekly* like it's your religion, your best friend is still your only real friend. Jesus, Ally, the world's blown up around you and you haven't noticed . . . Your daughter is living with another woman. Fleur hasn't seen her sons in years. She doesn't even know where they are and the two of you go on playing tennis as though nothing had changed. It's bloody weird. Maybe I'm to blame for Jane, the way she is, I had more to do with her in her teens than you did, but, Ally, you stay down here as though you're in a time capsule buried thirty years ago.'

'I do notice! Don't you think I worry about Jane, for God's sake? Fleur worries herself sick about the boys but what can we do? They're all adults. What can we do?'

Rowley closed his eyes for a moment then, in an oddly polite voice, he went on.

'Ally, I'm leaving you. I can't handle it any longer. I'm ashamed and I'm desperately sorry, but that's how it is.'

A funny roaring in her ears made her look down at the ocean where the waves were still idling in – so it wasn't the roar of the ocean.

'I'm leaving today.'

'Today?'

'Yes.'

'Where to? I mean, where are you going? For how long?'

'It doesn't matter where to. I'm just going. Permanently. I won't be coming down at weekends. I'll get my clothes and a few things. I'll leave everything else.'

He walked to the edge of the cliff, picked up a small stone and tossed it over.

'Don't, Rowley! Don't do that. There could be someone sitting on the beach down there.'

He leaned over and peered down.

'There's no one there.'

He came back and sat down, knees apart, hands dangling helplessly.

Big hands, she thought. They'd stroked her tenderly once, clumsily changed Jane's nappies; hands that hadn't touched her for a long time and suddenly she understood; said, with a gulp, 'There's someone else, isn't there?', sure he'd laugh and say no, in an exasperated voice, and he didn't. He nodded.

'She isn't to blame.'

'You mean I am?'

'You didn't do anything *wrong*. I tried to explain, Ally.'

'She's young? You're sick of me?'

The white edges the waves left on the beach looked like a lace cloth that wouldn't stay put.

'Ally, don't stand there staring at nothing.'

'I'm not. I'm watching the waves.'

'Are you taking me seriously?'

'Do you think I'm nuts? Of *course* I am.'

'You're making it hard for me.'

'I'm actually very shocked.'

'I've been trying to tell you for weeks. You always turned away or went to sleep or said you had to write to Jane.'

True, she thought, that's true.

'I'd like you to be rational about this, Ally. Let's be dignified, for everyone's sake.'

'Who's everyone? I thought this was between us?'

'You, me . . . Jane, it concerns Jane. Another person.'

He stood, walked backwards a few paces.

'Look out, Rowley!' Her voice was sharp. 'You're too close to the edge. It overhangs right where you're standing.'

Rowley moved cautiously away, went on: 'Ally, I love someone. It started three years ago. There's been a lot of pain. I thought I could walk away from her and I can't.'

She wished he'd go away, leave her alone, listening to leaves rustling, birds singing and twittering and the ocean sighing. She felt as though while he was there she couldn't get enough air into her lungs to stay breathing easily, a kind of rigidity affected her whole body. He was still talking and she wanted him to just bloody shut up and leave.

'Ally, suddenly I saw how little difference it can make to you whether I'm here or away. Your happiness doesn't depend on me being around. The things you do have nothing to do with me. Once I saw that, I knew it wasn't she, my lady, who'd broken up our marriage. And there's no hurry about a divorce . . .'

Ally hadn't got past 'my lady'. 'Divorce' didn't sink into her mind for a few more seconds and he was saying: 'We can arrange that when you're ready.'

'What?'

'Divorce. When you feel like going on with it.'

You don't go *on* with divorce, she thought, you *finish* with divorce.

'It's best for me to move out. I've made arrangements with Walt. You've got your car and the house is being put into your name and there'll be your usual allowance. There'll be papers for you to sign. Walt will explain it when you're ready.'

Walt was Rowley's solicitor and old friend. He had figured it all out for them. Three of them in it – Rowley, his damned 'lady' and Walt. It wobbled around in her head. Her role, the deserted wife. Rowley, the woman and Walt had decided it, readied the scheme for presentation to dumb, dopey Allys June, *Women's-Weekly*-reading Allys June, wearing out-of-date, wrong-colour lipstick. She watched a column of black ants deviating laboriously round her foot.

'I'm sorry it finished like this, Ally. I'll keep in touch, of course. I honestly think you'll find it doesn't make much difference to your life.'

How could he say that, how could he be so stupid and callous?

'Who's going to tell Jane?'

'I'll write to her today.'

Firing from the pit of her stomach came the relief of rage; lovely, bright-red rage. She wanted to scream four-letter words at him, like, how long have you been effing the bitch, that effing bitch? Effing her? She was so un-with-it she didn't even have the aggression to think the word, let alone say it. Hah, didn't she just?

Breathlessly, she asked: 'How long have you been fucking her?' Only, she lost her voice and the words came out as a feeble squeaking.

'What? How long have I what?'

'Nothing. It doesn't matter.'

How could she stop being angry just like that? She just felt tired, needed to lie down somewhere and go to sleep, couldn't go home where she longed to be because he was going there to pack his things and she didn't want to be around when he did that.

'Rowley, just go, will you? I don't want to talk about it any more.'

He looked uncertainly at her.

'You haven't had any breakfast.'

Worried that she hadn't eaten! Then he said: 'Well, all right, if you don't mind, I'll go . . .'

Don't mind! He was the fool, not she. A brief hope came. Was Rowley going through the male menopause? Men were said to have it now. Menopause; men, oh pause, before you leave your faithful wife. Men o'paws. She giggled. Rowley looked at her uneasily.

'It's all right. I was just wondering if you're menopausal, Rowley.'

Men, a pause'll make you change your mind. She exploded into mirth.

'Ally, I'd like you to come back to the house with me.'

That's right, he never could handle hysteria.

'Rowley, just piss off, OK?'

She'd never before told someone to piss off; she felt quite powerful. What a splendid phrase. Maybe that's what cats hissed at each other. Piss off, puss!

'Ally, I'd hoped so much we could part in a friendly way, not being abusive.'

'You know, Rowley, I'm just realising that you're quite a dickhead.'

From memory-depths, words were rising like small black balloons, words she'd chastised Jane for using, that Fleur's boys and their friends used to say. Rowley went quite red in the face and walked firmly away. Where the track dropped down between two leaning banksia trees, he turned.

'We'll talk again if you want, when you're calm. I don't want you to be bitter.'

Ally's voice became rough and harsh. 'Why don't you just eff off, Rowley?'

Damn, why couldn't she say that word? Anyway, he effed off all right, so fast he lost his balance and slid dangerously down the track, grabbing at clumps of tussocky grass. He pulled himself to a halt while she gazed meanly down at him, shaking with malice.

'Rowley, before you go, I want to know who she is. I'm going to feel stupid when people ask me and I don't know.'

Rowley started off down the track again. She yelled: 'I mean it, you shit! Tell me who she is!'

He grasped the slender trunk of melaleuca to halt his downward plunge.

'All right. I never would have thought you'd go on like this, Ally. You're behaving like a fishwife.'

And there was a funny old word. Hadn't heard it since her father snapped it at her mother when, on some rare occasion, she'd raised her voice to him. She looked down on Rowley and he looked sadly up at her. From the trees behind her a man came walking, nodded his head, said pleasantly, 'Lovely morning, isn't it?' went down the path. He said, 'G'day, how you goin', mate?' to Rowley, who leaned in against his tree to let him by. Ally and Rowley stayed staring silently at each other.

'I'll phone you tomorrow, Ally,' he said finally. 'I've always admired your style, Ally, please don't destroy that.'

A feeling rose in her chest that she visualised as a short, black stump, almost choking her.

Rowley went on: 'Come back with me now. This is absurd, trying to talk like this. Of course you should know who she is. Come back to the house with me, dear.'

It was 'dear' that did it, the paternalism of it.

'I'm not coming back to the house until you've gone, you bastard! I just want to know who she is. What's so difficult about that?'

Rowley let go the tree and slithered on down.

'You've been fucking her for three years,' she shrieked, 'why the mystery, what's her damned name?'

He reached the bottom and turned to stare up at her again. She thought, this can't be happening, like watching him drift away in a boat with the anchor chain broken while she wailed from a lonely shore. Tears spilled down her cheeks. She wanted to say, I love you, wanted him to forget what she'd said. This was no mere squabble. Rowley didn't love her. He was going away with someone else.

'Tell me her name, Rowley.'

He stood there and madness seized her again. She hefted a rock as big as a football, held it aloft.

Rowley crouched and protected his head with his hands.

'Are you insane, Ally? All right! If you want to know, it's Verna. *Verna.*'

'Who?' she said weakly.

'Verna.'

'Verna Ross?'

Her legs collapsed under her and she sank to the ground. Had he surged up the path and punched her she couldn't have been more devastated. The fight drained out of her and she longed to be able to take back the ugly little words she'd hurled at him. Verna Ross was such a *lady*, someone she'd deeply admired, of a pattern she'd like to have been fashioned to herself. No vapid, beautiful blonde was Verna, but a childless widow in her forties, beautiful, powerful, political. They'd be perfect together and everyone would take the relationship seriously and respectfully. There'd be no sniggers and little gossip, passing pity for Ally and no one would blame Rowley or Verna. No one, not even Ally.

Verna would never shriek four-letter words at anyone, let alone her husband. Ally felt ill. Walking on an empty stomach always nauseated her and fights made her vomit, always had. She wanted to be sick and could only dry-retch.

How long would it take him to pack and go? She never wanted to see him again. She'd never see *anyone* again, she'd curl up and die or something. For a long time she waited on the headland. Then she went slowly home. He'd gone. After all, she wasn't hungry. She scraped the egg on toast into a bin, drank three cups of black coffee instead. The day stretched before her, empty to the edge of sight. She was used to being alone; days had never done this before, looking like some strange, impenetrable territory.

She was waiting for something to happen. Nothing did. It was as though someone had slipped a glass bell over her. Suspended animation. Put on hold. Don't disturb.

For three days she walked around, waiting. How could most of her life just finish like that, with half an hour of words, then silence descending?

What was going to *happen* to her?

On the fourth day, the phone rang, the sound making her jump with fright. It was Jane. Rowley had written to her, as he'd said he would.

Jane was upset; should she come home? Ally said no, don't do that, she really was fine, shrank at the thought of seeing anyone close to her. Jane kept asking questions, she sounded anxious. Ally started to crack up, trembling violently.

'Darling, I have to go. I've got lots to do. I'm all right, truly. Don't worry. Goodbye for now. I'll write.'

Her head felt light. The brief conversation with her daughter had made her feel worse. She'd eaten little since Rowley left. The days were still elongating in a way that terrified her. Rowley had been right about her lack of friends. Fleur was the only one. There were acquaintances, people who exchanged smiles, nods and waves in passing, or chatted for a few moments when encountered. Why had she never made friends? It surely wasn't normal to have only one? She'd always skimmed past the lack, thinking it was because Rowley was in the city so much, never became involved in local affairs, so they didn't meet people as a couple and people didn't invite you out as a single.

Rowley, she thought, had plenty of friends in and around the city. She'd never known what he did there, nights. Why hadn't she asked? Why hadn't she cared enough to ask?'

Yet she'd thought herself content, normal, had kept busy – doing *what*, for God's sake? – days hadn't dragged. It was bad luck Fleur was away holidaying, or perhaps it wasn't. She didn't feel like talking to anyone.

It wasn't just the way each day had lengthened – thinking an hour had gone by, she'd look at her watch and see with horror that only five minutes had passed – it was the prospect of all the other incredibly long, empty days ahead of her, weeks, months and years of them. When she considered that, she felt as though her heart shrank to the size of a baby's fist.

She found a bottle of sleeping tablets in the bathroom cabinet, almost full. Did Rowley . . .? No, not even subconsciously would he figure she might take them.

Now and then, after some business deal and a week of excitement, he'd be unable to switch off when he came home for the weekend. He hated not to sleep so he kept pills handy. That night, Ally took one and woke next day feeling refreshed. She decided to go shopping. After a while, she lost the urge. For lunch she picked at canned fruit, at dinnertime looked at sardines on toast before putting them in the bin.

A few days later she was feeling quite strange. As she walked, her footsteps seemed to echo in her head as though the top part of her had turned into a cavern. Once she got used to it, she rather liked the sensation.

Then she did something quite odd; at ten in the morning of one of those stretched days, she swallowed a sleeping pill and fell asleep, to wake after dark, elated that a day had passed, feeling she'd outwitted an enemy.

The pills lasted for three weeks. Some days she felt dopey and slept without one. She seemed to have lost a lot of weight and her skin looked spotty. She thought of going to the doctor for more pills but couldn't face the prospect of explaining why she needed them.

Nobody came to see her. She had a card or two from Fleur. Occasionally Jane phoned. She was grateful to the ocean for its sound and movement. She couldn't concentrate on television and radio reception was always poor so she seldom listened to that, not even the news. She tried listening to music and after a while realised she hadn't heard a note.

On a Friday she discovered that the pantry was almost empty. It was an incredible effort to get ready to go out. She stammered when the girl at the check-out in the supermarket passed a casual remark.

She passed a cake shop and saw chocolate cakes. On impulse she went in and bought one.

She ate chocolate cake for lunch and again for dinner, had never tasted anything so delicious. She went out next day to get another one. The woman said they made them only for the Friday trade. So, all right, she'd bake one. That passed the time nicely. She became interested in cooking, absorbed in finding recipes she hadn't used in years, for pikelets and scones – eating them hot, dripping with butter and honey – fruit cake, puddings, custards.

Time had speeded up. She forgot about the way it had dragged before. Her breasts began feeling fuller and suddenly she remembered the way she'd felt when she nursed Jane. Her bras cut into her flesh so she discarded them. Soon, when she went shopping, she had to wear a floppy shirt over skirt or slacks with the top button undone. Zips developed a habit of creeping down. Briefs popped elastic.

All right. She'd been too thin before. She'd lost so much weight straight after Rowley had gone. Shopping for new clothes would be something to do. She was astonished to discover that size twelve no longer fitted. She moved up to size fourteen and a saleswoman strolled up and looked at her doubtfully.

'They might be a bit small. Would you like to try a sixteen?'

Bitch! She'd never been a sixteen in her life! Furious, she left the shop.

In the bathroom at home the scales loomed. With one foot she slid them behind the door. Ally began leaving curtains drawn and blinds down. She never confronted herself in a mirror now. Her brain seemed to have malfunctioned. She felt she should be thinking about what had happened, that some profound reaction to the change in her life should be taking place and yet she couldn't think coherently, would sit for hours with a book or magazine on her lap, never turning a page. She no longer walked on the beach or swam and that grieved her, yet she couldn't make herself go down the steps and through the trees.

Ally became anxious. At night, on the edge of sleep, something would come rushing at her like an unlit express train and she'd be sitting up with a painfully thumping heart. She had a premonition of approaching doom. When she dozed, it was to awake from nightmares and, when dawn came at last, she'd sink back, depression overwhelming her.

At five in the afternoon she began drinking whisky, gulping it down trying not to taste it. She'd never found any drink she really enjoyed. Rowley had left odds and ends of liquor and she was just finishing off the bottles. It took very little to lift her spirits and late afternoon became her happy time. After a while, she had to drink more, of course, to reach euphoria. A certain level after that and she was weepy. One night she took one more drink that pushed her past weepy to mean.

She set off around the house, talking loudly to herself, smashing, slashing and hammering at those items Rowley had thoughtfully left behind to adorn her home.

The tall vase in the hall went with a satisfying crash. His little collection of silver and pewter cups from schooldays and golf tournaments proved a problem, almost indestructible.

Next day she wept at what she'd done. Not nice, Ally, not nice at all, she thought.

After the spirits had gone she turned to the wine, woke one morning to find herself still a little drunk, and that frightened her. But then everything frightened her now. Still, when the grog was finished she didn't buy any more, so thank heavens she wasn't an alcoholic. That could have been nasty.

At last Rowley rang. She gripped the phone tightly.

He said: 'Sorry I haven't been in touch.'

'That's all right, Rowley. I didn't realise you hadn't phoned. I'm out such a lot.'

How expertly she lied to him and how relieved he sounded.

'Oh, that's good. I'm so glad you're keeping busy.'

'Oh, *sure*. I keep very busy, Rowley.' She was afraid he'd come to visit her, so she added: 'I'm going down to Tasmania tomorrow to stay with Fleur and her mother. She says it's lovely down there at this time of the year.'

That took care of Rowley.

She was almost living in the kitchen by now, except for brief forays to the supermarket; she craved sweetness. She ate a lot and had taken to sugaring her tea and coffee heavily. Occasionally, she noticed that her stomach seemed to be bulging and sometimes it felt as though her arms and legs didn't belong to her. Often her breathing came fast and deep, then she'd get dizzy and have to hang on to something until it passed. One day, she blacked out. Vaguely she thought of going to have a check-up but never got around to it.

One morning she was brushing her teeth when the curtains fell from the bathroom window, the rod landing in the bath with a clatter. Light poured in. Blinking, she saw herself in the mirror over the basin.

And there she was. Dadah, dadah! Let's hear it for Allys June, who has bushy, tacky hair, unplucked eyebrows and rheumy eyes. The skin of her face looked... pudgy and pale. How could this be? She'd always been lean, usually tanned, never, never fat and dishevelled. She ran, ah no, she didn't run, she *lumbered* for a chair so she could hang those rotten curtains up again. She sat on the bed afterwards, disoriented. The only reason she didn't plan immediate suicide was that she couldn't bear Rowley or Jane to see her like that, and one of them would have had to identify the body.

Ally began to laugh hysterically. They'd be so mystified and they'd say no, this isn't Allys June Esterwood.

Ally made an effort to concentrate her thoughts. There were things she had to understand. Rowley was not coming back, not ever, and she had to adjust her life accordingly. Whatever happened in the rest of her life was up to her, and that could be another thirty years. She whimpered. She had to *do* something. She had to do it fast.

Whatever she did was going to be much harder to do as a fat lady. Why had she let that happen? An awful weakness overcame her and she was sure nothing was going to change, that she was going to sit there behind drawn blinds eating until she died from it.

Other women were deserted, people lived alone, some because they liked to. Why couldn't she handle it?

The day passed and another week. Every day she woke up determined to start a diet and exercise programme, ate and sat around instead. She was sitting in the kitchen and it was almost dark and she hadn't turned on the lights. Someone came to the door. Someone walked into the house and into the kitchen and Rowley was saying, 'Ally, are you at home, Ally?' and the light went on. Rowley was there, staring at her.

She had on a faded housecoat. She put up a shaking hand and touched her hair.

'How dare you walk in without knocking, Rowley? How dare you come without phoning to see if it's convenient?'

It was funny. Until she spoke, she was sure Rowley hadn't quite realised it was her. He must have been standing there, embarrassed, thinking she'd rented the house to some fat slut, an old auntie he'd never heard of, maybe. There he stood immobilised, as though she'd aimed a gun at his head.

He backed off.

'Sorry. I'm sorry. I shouldn't have barged in.'

A look of stark horror in those lovely eyes of his; many expressions she'd seen in Rowley's eyes, never horror before.

It frightened her into shouting at him, nasty stuff, irrational. She didn't find out why he'd come to the house that night . . . he didn't get a chance to tell her. All the time she was carrying on like a lunatic, he was backing away, until he stood at the door. She hung her head, listened to the sound of his feet crossing the veranda, going down the steps, crunching on the path. Click, that was the car door opening, wasn't it?

Clutching the wretched gown around herself, she ran outside and down the steps, calling: 'Rowley, wait, I have to talk to you. Please, Rowley. I'm so scared. I don't know what to do . . . Rowley.'

Something about the way he was standing, the way he was clutching the car door, alerted her to the fact that they weren't alone. She bent until she could see into the car. A clean, light, fresh fragrance flowed into her nostrils, an arm came up and a hand switched on the interior light and in its glow she noted how slender was the arm, how long-fingered the hand and saw, too, Verna's hair gleaming sweetly like a little cap on her head, the winged eyebrows, the soft skin of her face, the clarity of the hazel eyes gazing at Ally so serenely, for a fraction of a second, until serenity fled and was replaced by shock.

From Verna, Ally began the same kind of retreat Rowley had made from her. A step at a time, feeling her way backwards until the bottom step bumped against her left ankle. She had a weird sensation that she'd discarded a quivering shell to wobble beside the car, while a white grub-Ally inched up the steps, across the veranda and into the blessed obscurity of the house where, door shut behind it, it listened through a tiny, white earhole to the diminishing sound of the car engine. Then the white grub oozed itself under the shower, scrubbed and rubbed until it turned red raw. Finally, it slid between sheets, closed its eyes and cleverly vanished.

Two

In the valley, people said, if you were going to have a terminal fight with your best friend, it'd happen in the hot, humid weeks after the spring storms had eased, before the summer rain began.

Sometimes, in the stillness, Jane felt as though she was slowly being crushed in the jaw of a tightening vice. She and Marjorie had been irritable, arguing monotonously over trivial things.

They'd driven into the township and Marjorie had gone to have her hair trimmed while Jane phoned Ally. Her mother sounded fragile. Funnily, that reassured Jane, who felt it was more normal than hearing that bright, brittle voice from a thousand miles away. Until now, Ally had been too happy-sounding to be real. It had made Jane acutely uneasy, because, while she could tell herself Ally was all right, handling it well, deep down she knew she was probably having a bad time, trying to adjust to what had happened.

Yet the thought of being with Ally made her curl up inside. What would they say to each other? If she'd been a stranger, come to her for counselling, Jane could have established a rapport quickly enough; but what was the use of going all that way to confront her mother over a gap of understanding as profound as the Grand Canyon?

It would have been different if they'd ever been able to discuss things like sexuality and Jane's right to make choices. Ally had an incredible skill for fending off things she didn't want to acknowledge. And perhaps Jane had been too quick to give way before that invisible barrier.

Marjorie was walking towards her. Her hair was very short this summer. There was nothing to distract from what Jane saw to be the perfection of her face; something so *pleasing* about Marjorie's face.

Jane was waiting in the shade of a gigantic jacaranda, dry, dead blossoms around her feet. Intent on some thought, Marjorie hadn't noticed her yet. The skin of her face was smooth, bronzed by the sun, perfectly held by the bone structure beneath, the cheekbones high, taut skin hollowed a little, then smoothly rounding over the jaw line.

Marjorie had very bright, dark brown eyes and her brown hair was streaked with gold, the intensity of the sun's rays bleaching it as effectively as any salon.

Marjorie saw Jane, and her wide, precisely curved lips stretched into a smile. Jane felt contrite. It was Marjorie who was the good-tempered, forbearing one, Jane who was always thrashing around being a silly bitch. She resolved to be different, from right now.

'Do you remember Gillian?' Marjorie's voice was animated. 'She's in town. I met her just up the street. She's on her way to Murwillumbah and she's invited me to go with her. I'll be gone for a couple of weeks, that all right with you?'

'Yes, sounds great. Lucky you.'

Jane felt bleak, wondered why she hadn't been invited.

Marjorie raced her home, dashed around throwing a few clothes into a bag, then was off, trotting through the trees to wait for Gillian by the mailbox on the road. Gillian, she said, was in a hurry, running late. Jane was left feeling angry and resentful. Had she become so boring and dreary that Marjorie would seize any chance to get away from her?

Well, why didn't she go down and visit Ally while Marjorie was away? But the days slipped by and all she did was mope around, occasionally wandering to the river for a swim.

Floating on the soft cushion of sun-warmed water, Jane thought of her parents.

It had surprised her for years that they stayed together, yet, now that the break had come, it seemed inconceivable that finally they'd come unstuck. She'd been startled by her own feelings of rejection and insecurity. In walking away from Ally, Rowley seemed to have done the same to her and the resentment she felt was as much for herself as for her mother.

Surely Ally had become accustomed to living alone? It had been her choice to live out at the beach. How could they have expected the marriage to survive, he in the city so much of the time, her mother moping away, or whatever she did, down on the peninsula.

Jane wondered idly if Ally ever thought how it would have been if her daughter had done the conventional marriage bit, presented her with grandchildren.

How on earth had her father chosen the cool Verna for his new alliance? It seemed to her that, like an arctic explorer, he'd slithered from one frigid zone to another.

She'd always known of her mother's frozen spaces. It seemed to her that all communication with Ally took place across that big freeze. Communication between them had been restricted. How could you talk intimately across such a wasteland?

Night groans used to wake Jane. When she was small, she'd be afraid of the sounds, her bladder would go limp and flood the bed. Snatches of conversation were remembered years later.

Her father: 'Ally, I want you to *see* someone.'

Her mother: 'What's the use? I don't know what I'm dreaming about.'

Her father: 'I think you do know. Why won't you talk to me about it?'

Why hadn't her mother talked? Was there so little between them, these two who'd brought her into the world, that Ally just choked on whatever horror drove her dreams?

At fifteen, Jane began to have nightmares. Poor Rowley. Two of them, screaming and moaning in the night, Jane unable to say what *she* was dreaming about. There was no argument about whether she'd see someone or not. Quick smart, he packed her off to see his friend Max, the psychiatrist. When younger, Jane had thought of him as the Spychrist. Rowley drove her in one morning and she saw herself as though swinging up a vine to Max's den.

Irresistible, that vision of vines and dens. Brown, sparse beard clung dryly to a hidden chin, like parched moss in a drought-stricken forest. Bright eyes gazed at Jane as though through water in a shaded pool. Glint, glint, what's that on the bottom?

Max never fully met her gaze, it was glance, flick, glance, flick away, but then, when he asked questions about sex, his eyes looked like animal eyes flashing at her from slits in a cave wall. She had to make an effort to stop her hands from flying up to hide her own eyes.

She reflected now that the Spychrist had seemed to love his job for the dirt his visitors carried into that imaginary cave, thinking that after she'd gone he scraped into a small pile what she'd contributed, hiding it beneath scraps of grass.

Then, at the end of the day, he'd pull thorny bushes across the entrance to the cave so no one could infiltrate and, puddling with his hands, he'd mix it all up – lumpy little bits of rape, incest, fetish, obsession, hers in with the rest.

She'd have felt mean and guilty about her Max-fantasies but for the fact that, on her third visit, he gently, almost absent-mindedly, raped her, removing her blue flannel coat, hanging it over the back of a chair, unbuttoning her blouse, slipping away her skirt, teasing down her panties.

He guided her backwards to the leather couch, thoughtfully spread with a soft, warm rug. She'd mentioned an aching back, and thought confusedly he was about to massage it.

When he removed his shoes, but not his red-striped, grey socks, his trousers, but not his shirt and grey cardigan, she became horribly embarrassed. All the time he talked softly to her, but the words penetrated only the outer skin of her awareness. Perhaps he meant to demonstrate that copulation was nothing to be afraid of but Jane never figured out what he was up to, really, whether he did it to other clients or was selective, overcome by her alone, round-eyed, round-bodied little teeny-bopper she'd been then.

When he withdrew and modestly retired behind a door in the corner (a gap in the wall of his cave), she heard water splashing (from a cavernous waterfall?) and a moment later his head appeared round the door and, like any respectable practitioner, he murmured, 'You may get dressed now, Jane.'

This she did speedily, then bolted down four flights of stairs, running all the way to Flinders Street station where she had to wait twenty minutes for a train, hands sweating from fear he'd come after her, forgetting that her father had told him she could go round to his office, so, if anywhere, he'd inquire for her there.

From Parktown station she walked to the beach and clambered around the base of red cliffs to a deserted bay. There she undressed with shaking hands, ran frantically into the cold water, rubbing her body with sand, diving deep again and again, until her skin was blue and chilled. Afterwards, she lay in pallid sunshine until her body had dried and she could dress.

She walked back to the station then and phoned Ally, asked her to come and get her. When Rowley wanted her to go for her next appointment, Jane fell on the floor and cried hysterically. Rowley's face paled and in a despairing voice he said she needn't go again. Neither of them asked her for an explanation.

Jane maintained a deep, terrible fury about the way she'd been raped. The violation of that young and tender body had shocked her intensely. For years her genital area felt numb, as though she'd been injected with a local anaesthetic.

Psychologically, the approach by Max had been so gentle, so clinical, so non-alarming and unthreatening, she now realised her bewilderment and confusion had created an inner schism, causing her to wonder if it had been part of the treatment he planned for her.

If some monstrous, faceless, male creature had pounced on her from the darkness, leaving bruises, blood, scratches, throttle marks around her neck, she could have screamed and howled, known exactly what had happened to her.

If she'd been close enough to her mother to stumble into her arms, pour out the horror of the experience, perhaps she could have talked out much of the anger and would not have been left years later with feelings of guilt that, because she'd never spoken of it, she was in some creepy way partly responsible for what had happened.

Rocking gently in the middle of the river, Jane reflected that her closeness with Ally had lasted for exactly nine months, during which she'd floated in her womb. After that, she'd been on her own. Sighing, she rolled over and swam slowly to the shore, picked up her towel and wrapped herself in it.

Every time she thought about the bloody Spychrist, she had a feeling that something buried was trying to erupt, like that awful moment in *Alien*, when a barely-glimpsed something burst from the chest of one of the astronauts. It was as though she had a little monster hiding in her body, a frozen embryo of a monster.

She should have had counselling after that episode. Instead, she'd never told anyone, had behaved, in fact, just like a textbook case. Why didn't I tell anyone . . . why do I feel guilty? Well, she wasn't going to tell anyone at this late stage, and I don't feel guilty, she thought firmly, walking up to the house in the trees.

Anyway, every time she brooded over it, some more leaked away, like lancing a boil and squeezing the muck out. Eventually, it would all be drained away and thinking about that little prick would be too boring to do. He was out of her reach. Once, she'd got to the point of going to confront him, only to find he'd gone. Overseas, she was told vaguely. Not expected to return. She hoped that by now he was dead.

The house Jane and Marjorie were renting had been the home of dairy farmers. A paper company had bought up thousands of acres of rundown farms. Where bare, grazing hills had once rolled across the landscape, a tall forest grew, reaching for the sky, a strangely uniform forest, destined for the pulp mill.

At first, it had been like living in paradise, waking on crisp mornings with frost heavy in the blue shadows of the mountains. Mist looped in fragile wreaths, snagged in every fold of the slopes.

In the spring, creatures began to stir, moving into the house. Yellow and black wasps with long dangling legs bumbled around, building layered mud nests. They had made Jane nervous, until she understood that the little creatures were quite uninterested in their human cohabitees, even politely deviated their flight course to avoid a collision.

One dawn, Jane felt a weight on her feet, and opened her eyes to see a dull black, coiled heap. As she stirred, the heap came alive, with glimpses of red, and a smooth head rose, with flickering tongue, bright, beady eyes reflecting light from lidless eyes. With a yell, Jane kicked like a stallion and the snake flew into the air, came unravelled, plopped to the floor and, with amazing speed, belly-danced horizontally through the open door.

In the evenings, as they sat at the table eating ravenously after a day of mountain climbing, two green frogs came trustingly, clambering over any foot that rested in their path. Jane had thought frogs would be slimy, found they weren't; they were cool and dry in her hand, though with a rather disgusting habit of jetting off a squirt of frog urine that smelt of mice.

Once, a frog departing from the kitchen window-ledge, took with it their nylon pot cleaner, tangled in tiny paws. They laughed helplessly until their chests hurt.

Then came the heat and violent storms; thunder that exploded over them rather than rumbled; lightning that cracked like a demon whip, left a smell of ozone, and seemed to sizzle through the house until one afternoon, with a terrified scream, Jane had thrown herself under the bed, cowering like a child.

The storms eased, days became still, hot and humid, no breeze stirring to cool the flesh.

Jane reflected that it was strange how Australians, most of them living on the coastline of their vast, island home, still 'went bush' in times of stress.

It was the timelessness, of course, that feeling of being reduced in size and, along with the dwindling, a reducing of problems that had been overbearing, overwhelming, within the environment of the city where people thought themselves to be all-important and natural life had been crushed beneath the weight of concrete and the glare of light.

Walking alone in the bush now that Marjorie was away, she felt in the silence a presence, some emanation from the land's past that held no hostility, no threat, only indifference, and that neutrality brought with it a kind of peace that penetrated to the very soul.

She felt better, calmer, lay on warm, hard earth in flickering shade, trying to extend herself into the peace of the bush, seeing her fears and doubts and insecurities as trivial. She went back to the house feeling strong.

When Marjorie came back, she thought they'd be able to do some solid thinking about the future, about the direction in which they wanted their lives to move when they returned to the city. The most important decision of all that had to be made was whether or not she wanted to spend her life with another woman. So far, her relationships with men had been disastrous.

For a long time after Max had so callously and coldly raped her, Jane had avoided men, not so much out of fear as confusion, so it was inevitable that, when she instituted her own brand of therapeutic intercourse, it would go insanely wrong.

She made what seemed to be a sensible decision to normalise her hang-up, by having an affair with a nice guy. Jane was living in a terraced house at Princes Hill. The nice guy's name was Rom and she met him at university where she was doing social welfare. He was OK. *Nice*. Handsome. Physically attractive. It was straightforward. They liked each other and Jane invited him home to her place with the express intention that he should make love to her.

If at the door she'd said she'd changed her mind, she was sure he'd have smiled ruefully and kissed her goodnight. At that point, there'd have been no pressure on either of them.

Her flat was pleasant, with big windows looking over a park. She'd been to Rowley's warehouse to select the furniture. There was seagrass matting on the floor and posters on the walls.

They'd been to a play at the Comedy, afterwards strolled several miles home. Poor Rom, it had started out a really great evening and he didn't deserve for it to end in such a manic foul-up.

They shared a joint. She walked casually to the bed and threw back the cover. Rom skinned out of his clothes and watched Jane get out of hers. Selfconsciously, she did a silly little bump and grind, while trying to suppress a sudden intuition that she was making a terrible mistake. Apprehensively, she'd become aware of dryness where she should have been slippery. Her mouth was dry, too, and her throat began to tickle. A paroxysm of coughing began. Tears spurting, chest heaving, she jerked her way to the kitchen sink, sipped a glass of water between bouts of coughing.

She wanted Rom to dress and leave. He seemed determined to stay.

Probably he was possessed of the appalling randiness common to his tender age, impatiently waiting for Jane to become still enough to mount. She sucked at a spoonful of honey, went back to the bed, shivering. He wasted no more time, lowering himself swiftly, chunky organ probing for Jane's hidden entrance. But due to her lack of cooperation, it soon dwindled to a softly pendulous, hopelessly inoperable chunk of flesh. There was an exasperated comment from Rom, that she might well feel responsible for raising it to a usable condition.

The mere suggestion made her gag noisily. For a moment it looked as though she'd have to make a dash for the toilet bowl, but then her stomach settled down again and she remarked angrily that such an activity would for sure bring on another coughing fit, something she was actually fervently hoping for, so that the whole damned exercise could cease and Rom go home.

Instead, penis erect once more, Rom valiantly had another go and this time made it. Three good pushes later he was crying out,

'What the hell have you got in there, a concrete mixer?'

Furious and embarrassed, Jane clenched her vaginal muscles, at which Rom gave a yell of anguish.

'Christ! Don't do that! Are you always as dry as this? It's not your first time, is it, for God's sake? Haven't you got some gunch you can smear around?'

She mumbled, 'No, I haven't. I've only just moved in to the flat. I'm not properly organised yet.'

'Shit, Jane, you don't have to be *organised*. It comes in little tubes, you know, not fuckin' four gallon cans.'

He was moving cautiously again.

'Are you sure it's not your first time?'

Jane shouted, 'Do you think I'm retarded? You're not the first and I don't know why I'm so dry. I can't help it. I'm *sorry*.'

A hand landed roughly on her right boob.

Rom said indignantly, 'Your nipple's like jelly!'

She tried to push him off. He held her down.

'OK. Take it easy. Just relax. It's probably something I'm doing wrong. What do you like?'

'What do you mean what do I like?' her voice quavered.

'What do you *like*? Want me to suck something, kiss something, rub you? How do you like to be worked up? Tell me and I'll do it.'

And of course, before she could be expected to answer, he'd lost it again. Rom climbed off her and walked to the kitchen, yawning, scratching himself lightly on the bottom. She pulled the sheet up to her neck while he drank a glass of milk. He came back and stared down at her, not unkindly.

'This has become a real challenge. It *must* be possible.'

Rom spat copiously on his penis, smeared the saliva around. Cold, frightened, devoid of passion, Jane asked herself why she was allowing this entry to her dear, shrinking body. She was being used. Not only was she a sex object, she had become a hammer-peg toy. At this random thought, she thrust her hands against Rom's chest. Nothing so feeble was about to stop him now. In thirty seconds he'd gone in, finished and, panting, was out.

Slowly she sat up. In the region of her toes a sensation began, sped swiftly upwards, erupting as a scream that almost raised the roof. It lifted Rom momentarily off his feet. Next moment someone was knocking loudly on the door and Jane was flat on her back with a pillow over her face, unable to breathe. Since the air in her lungs had been completely expelled by that extraordinary scream and she couldn't suck more in because of Rom's weight on the pillow, she began to thrash around frantically.

The pillow lifted, and he hissed, 'What the shit are you trying to do to me, Jane? Call out that you're all right. Go *on*!'

Instead Jane screamed again, although fairly feebly. There was renewed pounding on the door and a woman's voice shouting, 'Open up!'

Rom leapt into his clothes, switched off the light, flung open the door and hurtled through, one arm hiding his face, the other thrusting aside a woman who stood in his way. A moment later Jane heard a thud, followed by a thumping sound. The woman had her back to Jane, apparently watching something, then she turned and walked in uncertainly.

'Hey, listen, I live next door. You OK?'

Jane nodded.

'Afraid I tripped him. He fell down the stairs.'

Shakily, Jane stood up, wrapping the sheet around her.

'Oh shit, did he hurt himself?'

'He walked away. Limping a bit.'

'I feel awful. It was my fault. He didn't do anything wrong . . . are you sure he wasn't hurt?'

'I'm sure. He's quite nimble, actually. Made a good recovery when he fell. What happened? Did he rape you?'

'No! No, I invited him. It went a bit haywire. I don't know why I screamed like that. God, what an awful thing to do to the poor guy. He'll *hate* me.'

She pressed her hands to her mouth and started to laugh helplessly.

'I feel *awful*! I can't believe I screamed like that. He'll think I'm *nuts*.'

She noticed then that the woman was trembling a little and that she had very beautiful eyes, dark brown, set wide apart, with long lashes.

Later she realised that what Marjorie had done that night was typical of her style of going in boots and all. She could have just let Rom go by, instead of sticking out a slim leg and sending him crashing painfully down the stairs.

Jane always felt bad about Rom. Years later she saw him strolling down the 'Paris' end of Collins Street, Melbourne, a gorgeous girl clinging to his arm, a girl who wore a pale rose coat and a matching cap; her cheeks were pink and her eyes sparkled and she reminded Jane of a luscious strawberry. Jane and Marjorie were clomping along in jeans, boots and sweaters, just back from a skiing weekend at Buller. Rom knew her and pretended he didn't.

It flashed through her mind how pleased Rowley and Ally would have been if she'd taken someone like Rom home with her, if they'd had a daughter who looked like that girl.

Marjorie and Jane became friends, went to film festivals together, for long walks at weekends, to the beach in summer. A few times she took Marjorie to the beach house for weekends.

Two months after the night with Rom, Jane began to suspect that she was pregnant.

Nervously, she began taking very hot and prolonged showers, running up and down stairs as fast as she could, jumping from any elevated object she noticed when walking through a park.

When her second period after the night with Rom failed to come, she went to a doctor in Collins Street, chosen at random. After a brief examination, the doctor confirmed that she was undoubtedly pregnant. Jane made her escape as quickly as she could, muttering that no, she didn't think she'd make another appointment or do anything about booking into a hospital, because she was moving to New South Wales shortly.

Next day, she stayed in bed until Marjorie had left, then got up and sat in a chair thinking about the unexpected development. Why unexpected, she wondered? It simply hadn't occurred to her that her ridiculous encounter with Rom could possibly result in such a life-changing event as pregnancy.

For a week she said nothing to Marjorie about it, and in that time she could think of nothing but the baby forming inside her. It was the most amazing thing that had ever happened to her and slowly a feeling of delight possessed her. Rom was gone from her life, no need to consider him at all. The baby would be *hers*. She'd never had anything like a baby; not a dog or a cat or even a budgie flying around and landing on her shoulder, as other children were lucky enough to have. Her happiness grew until she couldn't contain it and then she told Marjorie.

Marjorie didn't seem surprised. She had, in fact, been watching Jane closely. She said calmly, 'So what are you going to do?'

Jane looked startled.

'What do you mean?'

'Are you going to have it?'

'What the hell else, for God's sake?'

'I just meant, are you going to keep the child or have it adopted?'

Jane was shocked.

'*Keep* it, of course. Jesus, it's not a book I borrowed or something.'

Marjorie cleared her throat.

'Well, I just meant it's a good idea to think these things through.'

'I have. I'm very happy about it. It'll be a nice baby. I'm not deformed or anything and Rom's a great-looking guy, you saw him. I can manage on my allowance from Dad.'

'Are you going to tell them, your parents?'

'Well, I'll have to, Marjorie, won't I? Not yet. I'll wait till it starts showing.'

Marjorie asked, curiously, 'How do you think they'll take the news?'

'Freak, of course. Doesn't matter.'

'No. I guess not.'

It was a few days later that Marjorie suggested Jane should move into her flat which was much larger than Jane's. It made good sense; they could share expenses. She'd never had a close friend like Marjorie, who'd become like the sister she'd never had.

Jane dropped out of classes and was glad to be alone in the flat when she vomited noisily in the mornings. Marjorie, sheepishly, began bringing home items of tiny clothing. Jane felt tranquil and secure; by three months the morning sickness had ended and she felt well again. Then one day, when she went to the lavatory, she saw a spot of blood on the crotch as she pulled down her briefs. A wave of terror overwhelmed her.

All day she kept going to the lavatory, squeezing out a few drops of urine, desperately hoping that the spotting would cease. It didn't. By the time Marjorie came home it had increased and she was wearing a pad. Her eyes were wide open and shining with fear.

Marjorie quickly put down her bag and the parcel she was carrying.

'Janey, what is it?'

'I don't know. Something's wrong. I'm bleeding.'

'Oh, darling . . . let's go.'

'Go *where*?'

'To hospital. You're miscarrying.'

'I'm *not*. I'm not going anywhere. I'm staying here. I won't go, Marjorie.'

Beyond the boundary of the flat, her home and Marjorie's, lay a hostile uncaring world into which she had no intention of venturing. Marjorie's pleading failed to change her mind.

For two days she bled heavily. Marjorie stayed at home looking after her. The bleeding ceased. The occasional small blood clot still came away, but nothing as big as those in the beginning.

'I'm so sorry, Janey. You really wanted that baby, didn't you? So did I.'

Marjorie had turned away to switch off the kettle and failed to notice the expression on Jane's face, so it was with complete confusion that a few weeks later she heard Jane say brightly, 'It's moving,' and looked up with a dazed face from the book she was reading.

'Sorry? What's moving?'

'The baby.'

Marjorie's eyes came alive.

'Hey, Janey love, you miscarried, remember?'

'I can feel it. It's like a little flutter.'

'You lost the baby, Jane.'

'It might have looked like that, but I didn't. I knew it was still there. I should know, shouldn't I?'

Marjorie squatted beside her, took her hands.

'I saw it, Jane. It looked like a small blood clot. It hadn't started to form.'

'What did you do with it?'

Marjorie hesitated.

'I didn't know what to do. I . . . flushed it down the toilet.'

Jane's pale face reddened.

'You mean you flushed a blood clot down the toilet. The baby's still there.'

Jane stared at Marjorie and went on, 'I think I know what happened. It was twins. I've read about this. Sometimes you lose one and the other hangs on.'

So Jane went ahead carrying her little spook baby, saying she could feel it moving, saying it felt like a big moth fluttering around. Her stomach obliged by continuing to expand. She wore loose cotton Indian dresses.

Five weeks later came another heavy flow of blood. Jane became hysterical. Marjorie held her hands again.

'There's nothing to worry about. It's just your period.'

'I'm miscarrying again!'

'No, you're just menstruating.'

'People have periods while they're pregnant. I've read about it.'

'Yes, I believe they do sometimes. But you know you're not pregnant.'

'I *am*. You don't *want* this baby.'

After a few days the bleeding stopped and Jane became calm. Her face became very pale and her eyes developed a fixed stare. She began to worry because the movements she felt hadn't changed to definite kicks.

Marjorie brought home a visitor, said brightly, 'Jane, this is Stella. Dr Robinson.'

Jane's skin prickled, her hands became sweaty on the palms and her legs trembled.

'I don't need a doctor.'

Marjorie said briskly, 'I'm just going for some milk. Back in a few minutes,' and whisked out of the door.

Stella was middle-aged with wise, kindly eyes, tall, a little plump, and the moment Jane met her eyes an extraordinary thing happened. Her stomach shrank to its normal size. She burst into loud sobs. When she stopped crying and could see again, she saw that Stella was sitting beside her. She said softly, 'Oh my dear, I'm so sorry. It's quite common, you know, but people don't talk about it much. It's known as phantom pregnancy.'

'But why? Why did I do that? I'm *intelligent*, I don't usually fool myself.'

'It's got nothing to do with intelligence and everything to do with love and strong maternal feelings.'

'I felt it moving, honestly I did.'

'Yes, I know. Normally you don't notice those movements. They're there all the time, mostly wind. I'm going to make you a cup of tea. You'll feel better soon.'

Stella insisted that Jane should go to her surgery next day for an examination, 'just to make sure everything's in order'. She didn't think a curettage would be necessary but suggested to Jane that it was only sensible to check everything out because, of course, she'd be wanting to have another baby some time.

Jane felt confused. She felt shame at her stubbornness and stupidity, and grief and disappointment threatened to overwhelm her, to wipe her out.

'Jane, are you all right?'

Marjorie's voice was gentle, her hand stroking Jane's back was soft and light.

Jane shook her head, mumbled, 'I feel . . . bereft. I feel as though someone has died.'

She felt stricken, and understood how parents mourn helplessly when a loved child dies, wasn't sure how she should handle emotions unlike any she'd known previously – intense grief, sharp pain, loss, worsened by the fear that what had happened to her must be the result of some inability to accept the reality of life, in which all events couldn't proceed as one hoped and expected they should.

That night, for the first time, Jane crept into Marjorie's bed, unable to face the rest of the night alone in her own. She'd expected to find sleep impossible. Instead, the warmth of Marjorie beside her was so reassuring and comforting that she drifted into it, awaking in the early morning to a feeling of intense desire she had never felt before, certainly not with the loathsome Max or with the opportunist Rom, yet there was no mistaking what it was.

She felt languid, yet was breathing quickly and her skin was tingling with sensitivity. In her sleep, Marjorie had turned towards her and one arm lay across Jane heavily.

Jane had wondered what it would be like to make love to another woman, had once dreamed that Marjorie was making love to her. She moaned softly, unable to resist the longing to put her lips to Marjorie's, gently at first, then with increasing passion. Marjorie awoke, responded at once. In Jane's body, a great convulsion began low down, spread until she seemed to quiver all over from toes upwards until she felt as though the top of her head had soundlessly exploded.

Marjorie kissed her, on cheeks, forehead, on the neck and shoulders.

It was extraordinary to Jane. She felt stunned that, after the shame of Max's invasion of her body, the fiasco of Rom's, she should so effortlessly, accidentally, achieve such perfection with Marjorie. She slept deeply again.

Later, she felt no embarrassment, only delight to wake once more to the joy of finding Marjorie beside her. She moved blissfully close, amazed by the sensuous comfort it was to feel the warmth. No wonder cats purred when they curled on a human lap.

She and Marjorie already shared so much, with Marjorie helping her catch up with the classes she had missed, endlessly discussing lectures and study programmes, enjoying the same activities in leisure hours. Together they studied, together they went for long walks.

Having once feared that she was frigid, Jane now gloried in the ease with which her body climaxed, as she explored with Marjorie the infinite possibilities of bodily pleasure.

That was the year their university days ended. Marjorie went to work at a rape crisis centre. Weary from the long grind of studying, Jane took a frivolous job as salesgirl at a department store. Before long, women she worked with began confiding in her.

'It's funny, Marjorie. They haven't got a clue I'm a qualified counsellor, yet they just keep telling me things.'

'You're a good receiver. You make marvellous eye contact, didn't you know that?'

Jane was disturbed to discover the problems hiding behind the seemingly composed faces of the women at the big store where she worked. Eye make-up sometimes concealed a bruise – 'bumped into another door' was a wry and standard joke – the bright smile that greeted a customer could dissolve into tears behind the scenes, as someone told her of depression that never let up. Many of the women were on tranquillisers.

'I'm looking for another job,' she told Marjorie. 'I didn't know there were so many people having hassles. I feel guilty not doing what I'm trained to do.'

Before long, she secured a position as social worker with the Health Commission in an inner-city suburb. The two women moved to a large, sunny flat in bayside Elwood, a block from the beach. From a balcony they looked into the sparsely-leafed branches of an ancient eucalyptus that had survived urbanisation and the tight fit of asphalt round its base.

Ally began to fly panic signals.

One Sunday morning, Jane and Marjorie sat on the lawn at the beach house with Ally and Rowley, revelling in the sunshine. Jane was idly gazing at a blue taffeta ocean, shallows and deeps patterned in light and dark shades.

Ally asked, 'You girls done anything exciting lately?'

Marjorie opened one eye and glanced quickly at Jane who said, 'I flew to Sydney for a conference but it wasn't exactly exciting.'

There was plenty of drama in Marjorie's work but she never talked about it, not even to Jane.

Ally went on, something timid in her voice.

'You never bring boyfriends home, Jane. Are we too square for them?'

Marjorie slid down in her deckchair, clasping her hands behind her neck and inhaling deeply. Ally glanced at her nervously and Marjorie said, 'Mmm, that sun's so warm. What about coming down for a surf, Jane?'

Jane said, 'The water's still cold, isn't it, Mum?'

It had always pleased Jane that her mother was an absolute freak about surfing, trim in a wetsuit, tackling the waves almost every day, year round. Jane had always known, vaguely, that her mother had had a sister who'd drowned at an early age and, somewhere along the way, someone had done a good job of defusing that memory in her mother for, far from fearing the water, she seemed to revel in it. Jane said suddenly, 'Mum, who taught you to swim?'

'To swim? Oh, Mum forced me along to swimming class when I was nine or ten. I used to be terrified, but she just kept making me go along and suddenly I could swim and I got over being so afraid.'

Nobody spoke for a while, then Ally went on, 'I'd really like to know, Jane, why you don't bring home any men friends.'

What was she trying to stir up? Jane felt she should now, right *now*, make a statement about herself and Marjorie, yet cravenly was unable to open the subject of her lesbianism.

'I mean, do you think it's a good idea for you two girls to be together all the time? It doesn't give boys much of a chance to get to know you, really, does it?'

Jane's toes curled under and gripped grass. Marjorie still lay relaxed, arms now hanging limply by her side.

'Oh well,' said Ally, 'it's none of my business, I guess. You don't want to leave it too long, though.'

'What?' Marjorie's voice was sleepy.

'Pardon?'

'Leave *what* too long, Ally?'

'Oh. Going out with boys. Thinking of getting married . . .'

'Mmm. I see. Not exactly *girls* any more, though, are we?'

'That's what I mean. You're getting older.'

'Do you mean go out with schoolboys?'

32

Marjorie was baiting Ally. One thing she detested was people referring to mature women as 'girls'. To her, it was the ultimate put-down. Jane jumped up and got behind Marjorie's chair, giving it a heave. Marjorie fell on the grass and squealed, jumped up and chased Jane. They ran down to the beach, shrieking and laughing.

'Hey,' said Marjorie, 'we're behaving like *girls*, that'll make Ally happy.'

Jane stood still and looked at Marjorie.

'Listen, I know I should talk to Mum about us. I will, when I'm ready. I'm not ready yet. Don't give her a hard time, OK?'

'OK. Sorry. Beat you up to the headland.'

Marjorie ran away along the beach.

Jane began to read everything she could find about lesbian relationships and not just relationships between women but between lesbian women and their families, especially their mothers. Wistfully, she studied one photograph that showed a grey-haired mother marching in a gay rights demonstration, in support of her daughter.

She read how realisation of their children's homosexuality upset parents, how some were unable to come to terms with it, how others came to acknowledge that they loved their children so much, they could accept the relationship as merely a difference in ways of loving, human to human. Not only the children came out of the closet; parents were coming out, too, in support of them.

Jane had sighed. It was she herself who was the stumbling block. How could Ally come to terms with it, if *she* couldn't take the first step of talking to her about how she felt about Marjorie?

Jane became acutely aware of mothers and babies. A young couple with a small baby lived in a block of flats next door and Jane found herself almost spying on them, watching as they hurried from the building, baby swinging in its carry-cot between them, getting into their car, safety-belting the carry-cot in the back seat and zooming off, the young mother looking back with a doting expression on her face, checking that the baby was safe and secure. Often, women who came to her for counselling had small children with them and Jane became easily distracted by them. She began to feel she was not working effectively any more. A vague depression began to fog her mind.

Unexpectedly, one morning over breakfast, Marjorie remarked, 'We could have brought up that baby.'

Jane was startled. It was as though Marjorie had seen into Jane's brain and correctly interpreted thoughts that to her had seemed muddled. Marjorie went on. 'Have you ever really thought about that?'

Jane shook her head.

'Well, you said Rom was a really nice man. I mean, I wouldn't mind if you got pregnant again, to someone like Rom. You probably wouldn't have any problems with a second pregnancy. Women do quite often miscarry with the first and go on to full term next time. What I'm trying to say is, if you felt like trying again, maybe we ought to talk about it.'

Jane jumped up so suddenly her chair crashed over.

'That's really freaky! I mean, that's *weird*!'

Marjorie swallowed a mouthful of muesli very fast and began coughing and spluttering.

Over the noise she was making, Jane shouted, 'Let's get something straight. I'm not a fucking incubator, Marjorie. Look, I'm not even sure what the hell I'm doing with my life, whether this is a lifetime arrangement or what.'

But Marjorie had grabbed her shoulder-bag and left.

For a few weeks, nothing more was said. Jane's depression worsened. She would have asked for leave from her job, but she couldn't think what to do if she had time off, and it seemed better at least to stay busy and depressed, rather than to have time on her hands and be depressed.

At night, in bed, she turned away from Marjorie or went to bed early and pretended she was asleep, and that was awful.

One night Marjorie walked in with a new hairstyle. Jane was whipping cream to go with a fruit pie. She looked up and saw Marjorie, her thick hair cropped very short. The beater in her hand jerked and cream spattered. Marjorie rushed to switch off the power. She began wiping up the mess and said nervously. 'What's wrong with you?'

'Your *hair*. It looks terrible. Why did you get it cut like that?'

Marjorie threw the cloth on to the floor, began to cry and ran from the room. Jane had never seen her cry before. She didn't come back until midnight and she'd been drinking. Jane, huddled in her dressing-gown, said miserably, 'I'm sorry, Marjorie. I got a shock when you walked in looking so different.'

Tears welled in Marjorie's eyes. Jane said quickly, 'And listen, that stuff about having a baby. If you want a baby, you have a baby. Go and get yourself laid. You're a woman, too.'

'I don't want to have a baby. I think you do. I think you need to.

Listen, I was talking to Stella and she said . . .'

'Well fuck Stella, too! She can mind her own goddamned business.'

'Jane, listen, don't be so angry.'

'I'm listening. You listen too. I wanted the baby I lost, that's all. I wish I hadn't lost it.'

Marjorie said softly, 'Some women have babies by artificial insemination if they don't want to make it with a guy.'

'For Chrissakes! When I have a baby, I'll bloody have it the normal way, do you bloody mind, Marjorie?'

And that Sunday, after she'd finished hanging out some washing, Jane stood limply, staring at the solitary tree, survivor of some lovely forest of long ago.

As though in a trance, Jane went downstairs, glided to the tree, stepping lightly across the humped asphalt cracking over its massive roots. She put her arms as far around the smooth, cool trunk as they'd reach, rested her forehead against it, then rolled her head from side to side for a moment so that each cheek in turn felt the tree. She became very still, leaning the length of her body against it. The sounds of traffic faded away. She heard the rustle of leaves. After a time, the tree began speaking silently, shared pain with her.

Jane developed a compulsion to hug the tree. Sometimes she sneaked down and hugged it while Marjorie was doing the washing up. She began to fear she was going nuts.

She also knew that Marjorie was right. She *did* want a baby, wanted it desperately, passionately, insanely, would go out of her mind if she couldn't have one. And how was she going to have one, when she didn't want a man to give it to her?

On a Saturday morning, Marjorie walked out on to the balcony and saw Jane clasping the trunk of the tree, crying bitterly. She sped downstairs. Jane wouldn't let go and couldn't stop crying. Marjorie had to drag her away forcibly.

'Janey, we're going away. I'm going to take you up to the country.'

So they left the city and the polluted water of the bay where they could no longer swim, left the sad gumtree for the narrow valley of the Bimdadgen river, where Jane now lay lonely in her bed, trying to understand what had gone so hugely wrong. It hadn't been that she needed more trees to hug, for she was surrounded by them and still she was depressed and confused. Why couldn't she think straight? Surely she could figure out what she wanted from life?

The more she thought about it, the more convinced she was that her problems started with the miscarriage. She remembered how she'd been unable to accept that the baby was gone, the way she'd encouraged her body to fool her, stomach protruding as though still pregnant, even thinking she could feel the baby moving. What was all that but a symptom of some deep dysfunction?

She *needed* a child. It was a basic human need. At twenty-eight it had begun to overwhelm her. She sighed deeply. The silence of this valley should have made it easy for her to think things out; instead it made it more difficult. Thoughts moved so sluggishly. Decisions became unbelievably hard to make.

So, OK. A baby meant the involvement of a male. Marjorie had talked about artificial insemination. What did you do for God's sake? Size some guy up for physical and mental fitness, then ask if he'd mind giving you a jar of sperm? There was a note of hysteria in Jane's giggle. She'd have to ask Marjorie. No doubt she had it all figured out.

If having a baby meant she had to get married, she would have to forgo motherhood. Right? Right.

Marjorie had said they could bring up a child together. They could. Right.

A feeling of surprise and elation came to Jane. The floundering had ceased and she was thinking constructively. It seemed to her that she'd made a considerable advance from her former state of muddled thinking and depression.

The question she couldn't yet answer was how to go about getting pregnant again.

Three

Never had Ally known such humiliation, shame and regret – regret that howled in her mind like a lost dog; remorse that she'd let herself become the creature Verna had observed that night, standing abject and pleading by the car.

Physically she was swept by frequent burning flushes, each accompanied by a shattering sense of unworthiness. She longed to be able to reverse time, wipe out that moment and the hours and weeks leading up to it, yet knew it was her own profound lack of self-esteem that had swept her on to disaster.

After days of pacing the house in disgust and anguish, she slumped on the veranda, legs thrust ungainly before her, gazing blankly at the ocean. Like the first small trickle of a turning tide, not recognised as the only positive thought she'd had in ages, it occurred to her that what she'd become was not only demeaning, it was incredibly, unbelievably boring. And *boring* was a wall that would seclude her for the rest of her life from anything of interest or value.

Was that what she wanted? At the horror that this aroused in her mind, Ally leapt to her feet and sent a wild yell soaring out over the trees. It ended in a gasping moan and, opening her tightly-shut eyes, she saw people on the beach below leaping to their feet and turning in her direction. She took in a long breath and was suddenly wracked by unseemly and explosive mirth, staggering into the house, tottering to each door and window, dragging curtains back, sending blinds rolling up with such force they spun at the top, tangling their cords.

In the bright light that flooded the house, she was dismayed to see how mildew had spread its spores, how dust lay thick, how mist from the ocean had mingled with it to spread layers of grime on windows and ledges.

She began making a list of things to be done. Staring through the window, she saw how lawns and flowerbeds were overgrown, neglected. Which should she start with, herself or her environment? Perhaps they went together? Fearfully, she acknowledged there was no easy way back from where she was.

Each morning, she'd make lists:
    phone hairdresser, beauty salon
    go for WALK
    do some EXERCISES
    GO ON DIET
and at the end of the day, she could cross nothing off.

Midway through one morning, acute revulsion attacked her so violently that she was nauseated to the point of dry-retching. On the way back from washing her face she ran to the phone and, with shaking fingers, dialled the numbers she'd looked up days earlier. In the afternoon, still shaking, she dragged on a loose cotton dress, got herself out of the house and into the car, where she had trouble getting the key into the ignition.

Then, nearing Parktown, she couldn't remember how to get to the street where the salons were. She had to stop the car and lean her forehead on the steering wheel, shedding weak tears of pity for her poor, messy self.

At home that night, though her hair had been styled, conditioned and blow-dried, her nails done, eyebrows tidied, legs waxed, after a facial and a massage, she still avoided mirrors. In the morning she looked only in a small ornamental wall mirror to comb her now shining hair. She *did* look better! She paused and looked again, cautiously. That day she sat at the kitchen table and worked out what she'd eat.

Even after she'd started dieting, she wouldn't get on the scales, not wanting to know what weight she was coming down from. After a terrifyingly short time of eating carefully, she was overtaken by a powerful urge to return to the comfort of the chocolate cake binge and suppressed it with agonising difficulty. Ally was appalled at the damage she'd done to herself, at the way in which food had now become a major issue in a life that formerly had taken little account of it.

After several weeks, clothes were fitting loosely and she was beginning to think about trying on one of her old dresses, walking more confidently, feeling lighter, optimistic, overtaken by a feeling that was near euphoria.

Sure, she'd regained control of herself. She bought a chocolate cake and, before she'd begun to put other purchases away in the pantry, cut and ate a slice. As she swallowed the last mouthful, she was astonished at the way the cake had clogged her mouth. She'd had to *gulp* it down. As the last crumbs were swallowed, she ran into the bathroom, and leaned over the toilet bowl while the whole lot was ejected forcefully.

Weakly, Ally put the lid down, sat on it and had a good cry. Even that became the subject of some kind of personal analysis; what kind of cry was it? Immediately she knew that she'd simply had a good cry because she bloody well *felt* like it. She realised it was simplest to keep only non-fattening food in the pantry. Pain, anger and depression became her dining companions; how could she live the rest of her life like this, for God's sake?

Occasionally there were horror days when she leapt into her car and drove off to buy chocolates and biscuits and ate them instead of meals. It was at the end of one of these that she began to walk again, determined not to return to the house until she'd walked for an hour.

The tide was in and the sand was soft. After five minutes, she was gasping, her legs aching, her feet on fire. Grimly, she forced her way through the sand. At the end of the hour, she struggled back up the steps and collapsed into a chair.

Slowly, day by day, the habit of walking came back to her. Some days, she didn't consciously feel like getting to her feet but her body was sending a different message, as though a second brain had grown and was giving separate instructions, urging the swinging of arms and legs, demanding the feel of a breeze in her face, the pumping of blood through the veins, the faster beating of the heart.

That was when she began to hope the battle was won, that her body was hers again, not a collection of bones and skin reacting to instructions from an unseen adversary outside her conscious self.

Gradually, she knew that she could again eat three enjoyable meals every day and still lose excess weight, as long as she obeyed her body and kept up the long, daily walk. At last she was close to stabilising her weight, reaching a normal attitude towards food again. Weeks earlier, too, she'd begun swimming each day. Even so, what the hell was she to do about the rest of the hours in the day? She attacked the garden ferociously, weeding, pruning, replanting, trimming and mowing. She'd restored order in the house and it needed little attention.

OK. That was all some people did, wasn't it, looked after themselves and their surroundings? That was enough, wasn't it? So why did she feel as though she was walking on the edge of a precipice, that one slip would send her headlong into a black hole that would ferociously suck from her the small gains she'd made.

If only Jane would come to see her. If only Fleur was back from her holiday. Yet she knew, with despair, that the company of others couldn't alter the basic problem, that she had nothing important or satisfying to do with her time.

She was sleeping poorly again, troubled by vivid dreams in which tidal waves engulfed her home, waking in fright to hear the full tide roaring on the other side of the trees. Once she dreamed of the canal along which she'd skipped her way to school, dreamed she'd fallen in and was drowning in a whirlpool, and woke with the sheet twisted around her body.

One day she failed to go for her walk and her swim, and next day walked compulsively for two hours instead of one, swam in surging water until she was exhausted, afraid of losing the discipline that was keeping her physically fit.

And then one day she was weeding in the garden when she heard a car turning in from the road. A cream-coloured Volvo drove up and a young man stepped from it, smiling. Ally stood slowly, eyeing him nervously.

'Mrs Esterwood? Ally? You don't remember me, do you? Ben . . . I'm Ben Maynard . . .'

He looked very healthy, with a tanned face and very dark blue eyes sparkling at her. He was dressed in expensive jeans and an open-necked shirt. Ally said, 'I'm sorry . . .'

'Well, it's been years. I took Jane to three or four dances one year. I went to school with Bim and Rocky . . .'

Slowly, Ally's memory turned up an image of a rather short, rather plump boy of fourteen or fifteen, Jane going off with him in Fleur's car, Bim – or was it Rocky? – in the back seat with a girl, on their way to a school dance. Was that Ben?

She said doubtfully, 'I remember somebody . . .'

'A rather small, stout person?'

The man was laughing. Ally smiled back.

'Was that *you*?'

He nodded.

'You certainly changed. And didn't you come from Western Australia? Oh lord, now I remember! Ben! Of course, I do remember you. How nice to see you again. Do come inside.'

She led him inside to the sun-room, asked him to wait while she washed and changed, then, when he heard her in the kitchen, he wandered through and sat at the table while she made tea.

'I don't think I ever found out why you came to school on the opposite side of Australia from where you live, Ben . . .'

'Family tradition. Grandad went to the college first, then Dad, and I was booked in as a baby. Bit silly, eh?'

'Oh well, as long as you were happy there.'

He nodded.

'Mostly.'

After Ben had left, Ally stood for a long time staring into space thinking, there is something quite terribly wrong with me. Why had the visit of a nice young man reduced her to such a state of nerves that her right eyelid had begun a weird little dance? She'd had to open that eye unnaturally wide, for fear he'd think she was winking at him. Her hands had shaken so much that Ben had noticed and said nicely, 'Let me pour the tea, Mrs Esterwood.'

'Oh, call me Ally!' she said quickly.

Why on earth had she told him Rowley was overseas on a business trip? Why did she have to be so evasive about it, when everyone knew that one in two or three marriages broke down?

The top two buttons of his shirt were undone, a thin gold chain lay on smooth, brown skin, with a glimpse of blond hairs, and she'd momentarily closed her eyes against a sudden vision of those blond hairs curling round his penis, which would be soft and silky-skinned, nothing about *her* to bring it to life. Then she couldn't seem to stop glancing at his chest; she was sure he'd noticed.

When he asked about Jane she'd babbled on about her social welfare work, said she was holidaying in northern New South Wales, a completely false image in her mind of Jane in a bikini lounging on some fashionable surfing beach, when she knew it was nothing like that at all. When Ben asked exactly where she was, she'd said she didn't quite know, only that she was renting a house in the Bimdadgen valley, up near Coffs Harbour.

Ben had been gently insistent, wanting to know how to get there. It turned out that he was determined to see Jane again before he went home.

He'd gone to the car for a map and said he could zap up the coast highway and, after he'd seen Jane, he could go up over the mountains to the Oxley highway and (tracing with his finger), on the Newell to Narrandera and head off on the Sturt, which would take him to Adelaide and back on course for the long drive across the Nullarbor desert to Perth.

Ally said, 'That's a terribly long way, isn't it?'

'Oh yeah, but I like driving and I'm due for a bit of a break. I really want to see Jane again.'

'Are you married, Ben?'

'Not any more, Ally. I was, but it didn't work out. I've got two great little sons, though, and my ex and I are quite good friends. The boys spend a lot of time with my parents – I live with Mum and Dad – so it works out just fine.'

Ben took out a wallet and showed her pictures of his parents and his sister and her family, his sons and his ex-wife, the lovely mansion on the Swan river, everything so beautiful and well-ordered. There was something very orderly about Ben, too.

They'd talked about Fleur and he'd said how disappointed he was to call at her address and find nobody there. He asked about Fleur's sons – that had been awkward, too. Or made awkward by *me*, she thought despairingly. Why couldn't I have just been honest and said, 'Last time Fleur saw them they were hooked on heroin'? It happens to a lot of young people, he'd have understood.

That night she dreamed of Ben. Ben, naked and fleeced with thick golden hair, making love to her. She woke soft and warm and sprawled, smiling, then, fully awake, guiltily she pulled the bedclothes around herself, lonely, lonely, lonely. What was she going to do about sex? Even though she and Rowley had made love so rarely over the last years they were together, the possibility was there. She wasn't cut off from it completely. So what did she do about that? It was something more for her to worry about.

She sat on the beach, legs hunched up, arms round them, thinking of her childhood. Her hand went to her face, moving over the smooth skin, feeling for the faint scar that could be seen now only in a very bright light at a certain angle. For years at a time she never thought of it, then one day a certain fall of light would highlight it for a moment. She'd had it since her earliest recollection, from a bad-tempered ginger tom cat that belonged to a neighbour. It had happened the day she'd gone through the gap in the paling fence – silvery grey, rough wooden fences of her childhood, palings loose – to play with her friend next door.

Importantly, the girl – Rosie? Roma? – had led the way into a bedroom at the end of a long, narrow passage that gleamed with spots of coloured light from stained glass panelling in a back door. On top of the bedclothes in a brass bedstead lay an old woman with a long, sharp nose and pallid skin. Not quite three then, Ally had backed away nervously until her friend said, 'Help me put a blanket over her. She's so cold.'

In spreading the blanket Ally had touched the woman's hand. It had been the same sensation as when the iceman slid the big block of ice into the box in the kitchen and she ran to slide her hand over the front of it, just able to reach on tiptoe. Not until years later, of course, did she understand that the old woman had been dead.

Ally's mother had never mentioned anything about a death or a funeral next door and she'd never told anyone of seeing and touching the woman on the bed. From time to time she'd wondered how the little girl came to be alone in the house with a corpse. Perhaps the mother had gone to work or out for the day, and the grandmother had lain down to rest and died in her sleep?

She remembered, with a shiver, how the two little girls had played in that room, trying on funny old hats and coats, laughing and giggling. That afternoon, after she'd gone home for lunch, she'd picked up the ginger tom and, when she squeezed him too hard, he'd broken the truce between cats and small children by slashing her with a lightning-fast rake of his taut, muscular front leg.

That was the year before Beth was born.

Ally stretched her legs and stood quickly, momentarily dizzy and began to walk along the beach. She stopped and stared vacantly ahead.

She was running away again. She ran away every time she thought of Beth. *Physically*, ran away.

Ally shut her eyes and pressed both hands against her eyelids, rocked from side to side. Then she dropped her hands, opened her eyes quickly and looked anxiously to see if anyone else was on the beach. Slowly she walked home, so tired she could hardly drag herself up the steps.

What would have happened if Fleur hadn't come home the next day? Maybe something really terminal, like a total unravelling of self, a final descent into an incurable mental illness.

Breakdowns had always fascinated her. How did people actually go into them? Did they one morning wake and make a conscious decision about it? Turn face to wall, slow down their breathing, refuse to speak or eat? Hibernate? Did they *choose* to do it or did it simply happen? Would it have happened to her if Fleur hadn't come zooming through the gate in her bright yellow Gemini? Fleur leapt out, slammed the car door, dashed into the house, yelling Ally's name, throwing her arms around her friend.

'Why didn't you ring me? God, Ally, you look ghastly! Hey, why are you shaking like that? Did I frighten you, rushing in? Sit down, I'll make the coffee. Jesus, kiddo! Take it easy!'

And, over the coffee, 'I only found out about Rowley and Verna yesterday. Flew straight home. I couldn't understand why you hadn't been in touch.'

Ally sipped silently, then said shakily, 'I'm glad you came home, Fleur. It seems silly now you're here, but actually I think I was very close to cracking up, you know?'

And with Fleur there, it *did* seem silly. It was incredible how noise and movement in the house, Fleur's voice rattling on, the quick way she did things, had shored up Ally's crumbling thoughts.

'Oh, God, darling, breakdowns are the *end*. Don't ever let that happen. It's such a bloody bore coming out of them again. Anyway, you'll be all right now I'm home. You'll get over it. I did when that big bastard walked out on me. I know what it's like.'

'I'm not like you, Fleur. You're so active. I get stuck in a . . . a . . . a time warp or something.'

'Well, I'm here to unstick you, baby. I'm dying for a game of tennis. I've got my gear in the car. It's a gorgeous day, let's go and hit a ball around.'

Ally stared at Fleur. She'd been teetering on the very edge of

43

confiding in Fleur things she'd never been able to talk about, and Fleur wasn't on the same wavelength. God, she needed to talk to someone. Somewhere there must be someone who'd listen to her.

Fleur had her by the arm.

'Come on, upsadaisy, dig out your tennis clothes.'

She pushed Ally towards the bedroom and Ally changed into shorts and a top, got her racket down and some tennis balls.

She felt confused. How could she be contemplating a nervous breakdown one minute and getting ready to play tennis the next? And yet it was all right now. She stared out of the window at the blue sky. It was as though a huge black cloud had rolled away.

Fleur dumped something on the front veranda, calling, 'Here, duckie, this's for you. I know you always loved this pink and white geranium and look at it, it's gone berserkers while I was away, so I thought, seeing it grew like a mad thing, it'll be company for you. I'll leave it on the front veranda, eh? No good on the back, bloody salt kills everything.'

Ally felt better every moment. The relief of not being alone, of not having to listen to what her mind was churning out, fossicking around like a manic miner dumping loads of trivia, none of it mattering, not now that Fleur was home and she had someone to talk to.

When the phone rang next morning she answered eagerly. It wasn't Fleur but Rowley, wanting to come and talk to her. She said no, she'd really rather he didn't come around; the sound of his voice was making her feel shaky and sick. Agitated, she thought of how she'd been last time Rowley saw her. She had to convince him that she wasn't like that any more, and yet she didn't want to see him.

'Rowley,' she said, 'I feel ashamed that you and Verna saw me like that. I'm back to normal. I've lost weight and everything's fine now.'

'Good, that's the spirit, Ally.' Rowley sounded very relieved. 'I, uh, feel bad that I didn't come back to see you, but I thought you were probably best left to sort yourself out before I came again.'

That was a cop-out. What he meant, she thought, was that he didn't know what the hell to do about her so he just left her alone.

'Ally, is everything all right financially? Walt tells me you haven't been to see him yet. You will see Walt, won't you?'

'Yes. I'll go and sign those papers. I'm looking for a job, Rowley. I don't want to be a financial burden to you.'

Well, she *was* going to look for a job. With excitement she reflected that that was just what she was going to do.

'That's nonsense, Ally. You're not a burden. You've always pulled your weight. I'd be most upset if you thought you had to support yourself at this stage of our lives.'

'Rowley, what the hell do you expect me to do with the rest of my life? I *need* a job, I *need* something to do, it's not really about money.'

'Well, it's up to you, of course. It won't be easy to get a job, though. Ally, I'm going away. I'm slipping over to London for a while.'

Ally had a sudden vision of Rowley on water-skis, sliding erratically across the sea to London. She suppressed a giggle, mustn't upset Rowley, he'd think she was still bananas. Instead, she said, 'That's nice, Rowley. Say hullo to Verna for me.'

Instantly she was furious with herself because it sounded like crawling.

'Why, thank you, Ally. That'll mean a lot to Verna.'

After she knew Rowley had gone away, it felt rather strange. Jane hadn't rung in weeks and there was a sensation of having been disconnected from the lives of her husband – *former* husband – and daughter. Ally felt an overpowering need to assert herself, to be independent of them, without the slightest inkling of what she could do.

Fleur's visits and phone calls tapered off. Probably she had a new boyfriend. It was a pattern, and Ally knew from past experience that it would last a month, perhaps longer, and then Fleur would either zap off to stay with her mother or she'd pick up her activities with Ally.

Each morning now, Ally compulsively stepped on to the bathroom scales, first removing her nightie, checking her weight after she'd been to the lavatory and before she drank her first cup of tea.

Food frightened her. Though she'd not only regained her normal weight but had actually gone below it, she was still terrified that the slightest transgression would send her skidding on to the path that led to that awful, bloated body.

She began going for drives in the car, taking a thermos of coffee with her. In some quiet country place, she'd park the car and walk, perhaps to the crest of a hill, there to sink into a reverie.

She heard voices from the past, Beth's, her mother's, her father's.

Like a small bug, she sat beneath a vast saucer of sky upturned over rolling, darkening, grazing plains, beyond the Dandenong mountains. That day, she'd driven a long way and would soon have to return or be caught on the highway by darkness. Stretched flat on the grass, she dozed, catching the last of the sun's warmth.

'Ally!'

'Down here, Bethie.'

'I want to make daisy chains.'

How sweet that voice.

'I'm coming, Bethie. You start picking the flowers, I'll be there in a secie.'

Abruptly, Ally sat up, moaned, then doubled over, clasping her arms around her stomach. How could such *pain* still be there after so many years? After a few moments, she lay down again, one arm across her face.

She and Beth standing shyly, one leg of each bent coyly, a finger touching corner of each mouth, a voice asking, 'Just the two girls, have you? Oh well, never mind, it'll be a boy *next* time, eh?'

Never mind what that did to the image the two little girls had of themselves, thought Ally. Old bitch, whoever you were, and her mother not saying a word in their defence. A choking feeling rose in her throat.

'Dad, can I help you?'

'No, run along like a good girl, you'll get dirty.'

'Come on, Ally, your father's busy, wash your hands. Oh look, you've got grease on your pretty skirt.'

Nobody ever showed her how engines worked, how to replace fuses, tap washers, never let her fiddle with things or get dirty. That was why she was afraid to be on the highway after dark, because she still didn't know what to do if the engine suddenly stopped.

After Beth died, visitors who hadn't known the family long always asked, 'Do you only have the one child?'

Her mother would hesitate, then say nervously, 'Run outside and play, Ally.'

Eventually, Ally would be almost out of the room before her mother spoke.

What had her mother said after Ally had gone? She'd never tiptoed back to hear, hadn't wanted to, was afraid to.

She thought of her father's death. It was at the end of a hot summer. He was pushing along the heavy mower, metallic whirring of revolving parts, and Ally watched from the kitchen window as she washed dishes, her mother lying down, resting. The house was full of that thick silence that descended on it in the years after they lost Beth. She remembered her father leaving the mower and walking out of her sight; herself wiping the sink, sweeping the floor, squeezing lemons and taking a glass of lemon drink to where he sat on the veranda, head drooping on his chest, then going back to the kitchen, carefully pouring the drink back into the jug and putting it into the fridge because she didn't want to wake him. Later her mother found him dead, still in the same pose, chin touching upper chest.

That winter her mother sold the house and they moved to an inner-city suburb. Ally hated it. There were no open spaces. She learned typing and shorthand, went into an office job, met Rowley fresh out from London when she was twenty. His quietness appealed to her and her mother approved. When they were married a couple of years later, Ally was surprised at how well he got on with her mother who sometimes flirted very gently with him. Jane was their only child. That was rather strange. They'd never tried *not* to have another.

Ally had learned to drive when Jane went to school, she used to drive a lot, and now she was doing it again, aimlessly.

Once she drove to where they'd lived when Beth was alive. She couldn't find the paddocks, of course, for they'd been built over long since. It worried her, though, that she couldn't find the creek. It *had* to be still there. It was such a wide stream after rain. It couldn't have just vanished. She drove up and down streets and down lanes between rows of houses.

She found a bridge and parked the car near by, walked expectantly out, thinking to find the creek below. Looking down, she saw a vast confluence of concrete pipes, huge, echoing ducts bearing water rushing beneath the earth and at once imagined being swept into the darkness. They'd buried the creek. She fled.

One cold afternoon at home, she dived into the surf, longing for waves to wash over her, water to foam against her skin, for her hair to be plastered to her skull, wanted that salty liquid to siphon through nostrils, ears, eyes, mouth, erasing all. Afterwards, wrapped in her towel, she crouched against a rock, the roar of the surf obliterating thought.

She saw a man enter the surf. He went in and out again quickly and she knew he thought himself to be alone on the beach by the way he swung his arms unselfconsciously, ran on the spot, began walking carefully over a broad wash of pebbles stranded by the tide, placing his feet gingerly, hobbling awkwardly, his body sagging.

The man wore briefs caught tight across the groin, outlining his sexual organs. A big man, strongly built; an ageing man, stomach bulging just a little, looking vulnerable. Frailest and most vulnerable that cold-shrivelled penis and crumpled testicles, bunched beneath the thin nylon material.

Ally turned her head away and closed her eyes so that, if he saw her, he'd think she hadn't noticed him. Her father had worn woollen bathing shorts, fitting from waist to top of thigh and, after a few wears, the wool stretched and he used to glance quickly down, often turning furtively away to tuck in errant flesh.

She remembered him walking up a beach as she squatted on the sand, absorbed in the motions of a small crab which was trying to escape her probing finger. Looking up at her father, she glimpsed bluish flesh, dark hair curling around that private part of his body never before observed.

Ally moved restlessly and the man on the beach saw her. At once he walked chest out, stomach sucked in, as though concealing a weak, inner self, compelled to display to her the strength expected of him as a male. How often she'd seen men make that same quick bodily adjustment. She pulled the towel tightly round her and, as the man moved off towards the headland, was overcome by grief so intense it seemed to mushroom into the space around her.

She cried. For the man on the beach, for Rowley, for her father. For herself. Grieving, she was *grieving*. Ally stopped crying, stood up and began pacing along the beach. She was in a state of grief! That's why she'd been behaving so strangely. As though after a death, she'd had to work her way through the shock of Rowley leaving her, of the breakdown of her marriage, such as it had been. She wasn't going crazy. She was simply mourning something lost.

Sniffing, she wiped her nose on an edge of the towel. Deep in her brain spun a recorder, compulsively, relentlessly, storing all experiences. Something was observed in the present, up it came with a parallel from the past. Savagely, she thought, well, I'm dam' well sick of it, sick of swinging between present and past, as though some stupid, random-fingered dwarf scuttled in her brain, pressing buttons.

Out loud, she shouted, 'I'm sick of it, do you hear? Sick of it!'

Four

Jane had fallen asleep in the big squatter's chair on the back veranda. It had been a breathlessly warm day. Marjorie had been gone for a week.

The voice was male and came from inside the house, 'Hullo! Anyone home?'

She sprang to her feet, alarmed. Looking down the hall from the back door, she saw a figure looming.

'Hi. Jane?'

At least it was someone who knew her name. She'd had a sudden, acute sense of how isolated and vulnerable she was with Marjorie away.

'Who're you?'

He came out on to the veranda and she edged away, staring at the fair-haired man.

'You *are* Jane, aren't you? Sorry if I startled you.'

Slowly a smile spread over Jane's face.

'My God, Ben Maynard!'

There was no mistaking him, not now she could clearly see those extraordinarily deep blue eyes. He'd grown so much taller, although he was still only average height.

He stepped close and hugged her. Without flinching, Jane hugged back and they rocked slightly, both laughing. She pushed him away and looked up into his face,

'How on earth did you find me?'

'Your Ma gave me a clue and I just followed it up. When I got to the township I went to the neighbourhood centre. No problem. Hey, you've turned into a classy lady!'

'Well, you've grown up quite nicely yourself. Whatever happened to that tubby little monster I used to know?'

'Come off it, I wasn't *that* fat!'

'You weren't that thin either. You used to eat like a pig.'

'Well, I was homesick, wasn't I?'

Jane hugged him again.

'Yes, you were, poor little pet. Anyway, you certainly stretched yourself out, didn't you? What are you doing over here? I thought you went home to work for your rich Daddy.'

'I did. I do. That's what I'm doing over here. He's expanding into a mega-tycoon and I'm doing a bit of shoving for him in the right quarters.'

'Won't do you much good in this little valley, mate.'

'I'm on my way home now. This is my little holiday.'

'On your way *home*? You're like eight hundred miles off course, aren't you?'

'Just a detour to see my all-time favourite girlfriend.'

They went inside and talked while Jane put the kettle on the primus. Jane asked, 'Did Mum tell you about Bim and Rocky?'

'No, what about them? She was pretty vague when I asked what they were doing.'

'Silly little buggers got hooked on drugs. Last news I had of them was from somewhere around Cedar Bay, way up north. They were on smack by then. Fleur never hears a word from them. She and Mum are real little dinosaurs, you know. They just ignore anything they can't handle. It's weird.'

'Your mother was really nervous the day I visited. Must have caught her on the hop, I guess.'

'Oh, Ben, she was always like that. And I guess since Dad walked out, she's gotten worse. Fleur's her only friend and you said she was away.'

Jane paused, then went on, 'That's odd, I could have sworn Mum told me she and Fleur were playing tennis a lot. Must have misunderstood her.'

'What's that about your Dad?'

'She didn't tell you?'

'Just that he was on an overseas business trip.'

'Well, that's Mum for you. Stiff upper lip. No, they've split up.'

She looked fondly at him.

'Hey, listen, what about you? Married, kids, what's been happening?'

While he talked, she watched him. What a lovely, relaxed guy he'd become. A bit like Rom's style. Divorced, he was telling her, but no hassles, still saw a lot of his ex and her new husband, couple of cute little sons and he saw them all the time, took them yachting out to Rottnest and yes, he had a girl and it was getting serious.

Why not Ben? It hit her with almost a physical jolt. Why not *Ben*? – Ben, almost as familiar and comfortable as Marjorie. It could have been planned. Marjorie away, the two of them alone together. At the thought, Jane felt lust stirring. She could handle this. She wanted him! It was all flowing, she just had to go with it. Her heart began to beat rapidly. Take it easy, she thought, just relax and take it easy.

Ben was asking about her life; lightly, she said she'd been too busy studying to get really involved with anyone. She was here on holiday with another social worker. Her friend had gone further north for a couple of weeks.

Ben stayed for three days, and after he'd gone Jane knew it had been a beautiful interlude for both of them. She felt so good about it. There'd been nothing clinical about it, nothing calculated. She'd really wanted him and that was how it should have been; how could she have cheated her baby by not loving its father?

When he'd thoughtfully asked should he . . .? she'd said no, he didn't have to do anything, it was OK and of course he'd have thought she was on the pill or something. And it didn't matter that he was never going to know about this baby, because he had children already and he'd be sure to have more.

The only awkward moments had come towards the end when Ben had suddenly suggested they get married and she'd had to say, 'Ben, darling, I adore you, it's been so special, but it'd be like marrying my *brother*.'

He'd looked crestfallen, then grinned and said philosophically, 'Just as well you haven't got a brother if this is your idea of sisterly love.'

He'd been so sweet. Maybe he was even relieved that she didn't want any more than what they'd had. The girl over in the West was probably much more suitable. And after all, Ben and Jane . . . it was almost a tidying up, a catching up on unfinished business from their teenage years.

Early on the fourth morning of his visit, Ben drove away. She waved until the car disappeared around the first bend in the track, felt lonely when the sound of rocks rattling under wheels faded into silence. In the early dawn light he'd made love to her for the last time.

Jane stood there, listening to a whip bird down near the river, the long, descending whistle followed by the whip crack echoing and re-echoing. She went inside, stirred up the fire and made coffee. It had been so good to be with Ben for a short time and now it was good to be alone, waiting for Marjorie to come back.

She had a really wonderful feeling about Ben, with no regrets. She went into the bedroom and lay down, her legs propped up on pillows. This morning had been her last chance. She wasn't going to take any risks.

Late in the afternoon she drove into the town and phoned Ally. She was startled and pleased by the animation in her mother's voice as she told her of Fleur coming home, Ben's unexpected visit . . . Jane interrupted, 'Ben's been to see me. He's just left today on his way home.'

'He really got there then? I'm so glad. Hasn't he turned into a lovely fellow?'

Yes, my darling old Mum, he's very nice and I'm really quite sad I can't say to you that I'm going to marry him. How happy Ally would be if she'd been able to say that to her.

'He always was nice, Mum. It was terrific to see him again. He's like a brother to me.'

There, that should make it clear to her. It did. Ally's voice lost some of its bubble. She told Jane that Rowley had rung with news of his trip to London. The red light began blinking. Jane said quickly, 'Mum, my money's cut out. Mum, I love you.'

Had she heard? The dial tone had cut in again.

When Marjorie came back from Murwillumbah, Jane ran to meet her, smiling. Marjorie hugged her, then held her away and stared at her.

'You look marvellous again. Perhaps you needed to be on your own!'

Suddenly, Jane felt shy. Should she tell her about Ben? Why not leave it until she found out if she was pregnant? Let it be a surprise?

Marjorie was full of news, anyway, and didn't ask what Jane had been doing. She had made up her mind they should go back to Melbourne. All that year she'd been feeling burned out by her work at the crisis centre, knew it was time to move on to something else. Now she had a chance to become involved in establishing a women's health centre and funding looked good.

'If I want to be in on it, I'll have to get back straight away, Jane.'

'That's fine, because I want to go and visit Mum, anyway. I've been thinking a lot about her and, you know, I'm ready to talk to her.'

'About us?'

Jane nodded. 'Yes.'

It had, in fact, occurred to Jane that she must tell Ally about her relationship with Marjorie, about their plans for the future, because how could she hit her mother with news of a pregnancy and a lesbian relationship at the same time? That's what was going to happen if she didn't hurry up.

Although it had been only a few days since Ben left, Jane had the conviction that she was pregnant again.

'Marjorie? I want to have a talk about what I'm going to say to Mum about us . . .'

Marjorie interrupted. 'Yes, sure, good idea. But not right now, huh? Let's go for a swim.'

'You go. I'll start the dinner.'

Marjorie went swinging off down the slope, whistling. When she came back, Jane was singing softly as she slid a mushroom quiche from the oven. Fresh and glowing, Marjorie towelled her hair vigorously. As they ate, she talked enthusiastically about the women she'd met at Lismore and Murwillumbah, so much going on up there, a refuge established, rape crisis centre being planned.

'There's so much energy there, Jane. It was so stimulating and exciting. Gillian's got me fired up about the health centre. I can't wait to get at it.'

Afterwards they took a bottle of wine on to the veranda and Jane said, 'I really need to think carefully, how I'm going to explain to Mum about us. I know she's suspected how it is, for ages, and I think the idea terrifies her.'

'It's a normal reaction.'

'I know. I want to make it *better* for her, you know?'

Marjorie said doubtfully, 'You should try, of course, but be prepared for a split from her. She's not exactly receptive to new concepts, is she?'

'I know. Look, this is pretty ridiculous, but *I* need educating, too, Marjorie.'

'What do you mean?'

'Well, look, I've been with you for nearly four years. Before that, I guess I simply assumed that I was a perfectly normal heterosexual, with a few hang-ups about sex. I guess I'm as confused about it as anyone else.'

'About what?'

'About *lesbianism*, idiot.'

'Darling, what are you trying to say?'

'Well, you've never talked to me about yourself. I hardly know anything about you, before you met me, except that your mother got married and went to live in America before we met each other. But I don't know what kind of a childhood you had, what kind of experiences . . .'

Marjorie had been listening and looking puzzled. Suddenly she laughed.

'Oh right, I get you. You mean what turned me into a lesbian?'

'Not exactly that. Oh, *shit*, you're making me feel like some dumb, middle-class bitch . . .'

'You *are* middle-class. I didn't say you were a dumb bitch, did I?'

'No, but I can't help it that I was born middle-class . . .'

'Poor pet, I'm lucky, aren't I, born working class. Big advantage in the women's movement.'

Marjorie was still chuckling. She went on: 'You have to pretend you're working class even if you're not. Janey, what are you on about?'

'I want to know about *you*. You're so real and positive and energetic, everything just so right, everything you do works out OK. You don't hassle people and people don't hassle you. How can you be so sure of yourself. You're always *you*!'

'You don't think you're *you*, is that the problem?'

'Sort of. Though I feel better now than I did a while ago. I hope you're taking me seriously. It's important to me.'

Marjorie had stopped smiling.

'Of course I am. What do you want to know about me?'

'It sounds silly, but are you really sure of yourself, of being lesbian?'

Marjorie nodded.

'Yes. I always have been.'

'That's it! How did it happen? Being lesbian?'

Marjorie got up and strolled to the edge of the veranda, then reached for the wine bottle and poured a little more into her glass. She sipped at it reflectively.

'Funny. I've never really thought about that.'

She sat down and pushed a big cushion behind her back, pulling her legs comfortably into a yoga position.

'That's really interesting. Maybe it's because Mum never laid anything on me, never insisted I had to be particularly one thing or the other.'

'You mean . . . what?'

'She never made me particularly *girlie*, I suppose. She was an amazingly strong woman herself.'

'Where did you live when you were little?'

'Garden City.'

'Funny, isn't it? You lived in Garden City and I lived in Gardenvale.'

'I know you did.'

'I loved Gardenvale. When I think of it, I get all kind of warm and cosy. Marjorie, you never talk about your father . . .'

'I didn't ever know him. I haven't a clue who he was.'

Jane looked shocked.

'Why? How?'

'Well, Mum got pregnant with me on her eighteenth birthday. She'd never drunk liquor until then and she just sort of got drunk without knowing it. She suspected who the father was, she vaguely remembered it happening, but it was so, well, dream-like, I guess, that she just went away and decided to bring me up herself, long before it became OK to be a single mother. She was marvellous. Couldn't even get a pension then.'

'Doesn't it bother you, not knowing who your father is?'

'It doesn't. I know you're supposed to get all traumatic about it, but for some reason I'm not.'

Marjorie stretched her legs out and yawned, then lay flat on the veranda, thinking of how hard her mother had worked to support them.

'Nanette – my mother – always worked as a waitress, because that way she could take me to work when I was a baby. She was really good at it and never had any trouble getting jobs.'

'Did she have men friends?'

'Oh yeah, sure. On and off.'

'I still don't see what turned you into . . .'

'God, Jane, you don't necessarily get turned into being a lesbian, for heaven's sake. Some women know who they are, that's all. It's really perfectly simple and you're making such a big deal of it. You don't have to stay a lesbian if you don't want.'

'I do! I mean, not particularly a lesbian. I want to stay with you. I know that now. I'm sure of it.'

Marjorie looked pleased, turned her head to smile up at Jane.

'I'm getting awfully sleepy. Do you want to keep talking?'

'No. No, I think I understand.'

'I'm not sure you do. But never mind, I'm off to bed. I can't keep my eyes open. Been a long day.'

She stood up, took Jane's hands and pulled her to her feet.

'Listen to me. Until I met you, a few times I thought I'd found someone I wanted to share my life with, really share it, for keeps. It never quite worked out. I thought it was going to, with you. I think it still can, but don't let's push it too hard, OK?'

She kissed Jane lightly on the cheek and turned away.

Although she'd been sleepy when she lay down, Marjorie listened to

Jane moving around the kitchen. She yawned several times, closed her eyes, thought over the conversation they'd just had, and felt guiltily that perhaps she should have fought off her weariness from the day's travelling to talk longer with Jane.

How was Ally going to react when Jane finally talked honestly to her mother? Much the same as most parents, she thought wryly. Marjorie had been so lucky with her mother. Nanette somehow had filled the role of both parents so that Marjorie's conjectures about her father were limited to idle speculations about his physique and appearance. She suspected he must have looked much like she did, for, while Nanette was barely five feet tall, her daughter was six inches taller, with long arms and legs. Nanette's hair was fair and curling, her eyes blue – men were always attracted to her air of frail femininity. She was fastidious in personal habits and an almost fanatical housekeeper, doing the work so quickly and surely that she never had given the appearance of being hung-up on cleanliness. Always having to have a second job outside the home, it just seemed more sensible to live in orderly surroundings.

During Marjorie's schooldays, her mother had had only two relationships with men. Marjorie remembered seeing her mother, eyes blazing, standing at the front door of the house they then lived in, standing tall in high heels, holding the door wide open, flinging out on to the lawn a large suitcase, the lid of which flew open to scatter belongings and clothes. The man in her life had been leaving . . . what was his name? Morris? Austin? Something to do with cars. He'd gone very hurriedly, anyway, the door slammed after him and she remembered Nanette swishing her hands briskly together then walking elegantly to the kitchen to make a cup of coffee. That afternoon was the day she took Marjorie to the zoo, for no particular reason, except, she thought later, to be sure her daughter had a happy memory of that day. Marjorie clearly remembered the fearful delight of riding on the large, dusty elephant.

Nanette talked to her all the time about everything to do with their lives, so no doubt she'd explained Morris/Austin's going. She had no recollection of it now.

They'd moved then and Marjorie had come under the motherly wing of Mrs Funt who owned a high-class restaurant where Nanette was employed for years. For a while there was a man called Rudy, but one night he'd drunk too much and accused Marjorie of being cheeky and in the argument that followed he'd made a threatening move towards her. Nanette, chopping meat for their dinner, had gone for him with the meat cleaver. Exit Rudy, thought Marjorie with a grin.

Nanette was always completely in charge of her life and, with a mother like that for a role-model, Marjorie had grown up absolutely clear in her mind and sure of herself, her energies never depleted by rows with her mother. Men simply hadn't figured much in her life as she grew up. There'd been male teachers she'd looked up to, boys she'd played soccer and cricket with, until the development of breasts had embarrassed her. She just seemed to gravitate naturally to an all-women area when she left university and looked for a job. Women seemed to share so much with each other, always ready to explore new ideas, new concepts. Marjorie had never thought of herself as anything other than female, and remembered ruefully the time she'd had her hair cut really short, in some kind of foolish effort to establish or reinforce her relationship with Jane. Now, if it was short, it was simply because that's the way she liked it at that moment – comfort, simplicity, whatever.

Not long before Jane and Marjorie first met, Nanette had become interested in an American. In a startlingly short period of time, they'd married and now they lived in New York, seemingly ecstatically happy. Before they'd flown out, Marjorie's stepfather had deposited five thousand dollars in her bank account, ignoring her protests. It was to pay her air-fare any time she felt inclined to visit them. One of these days, she thought, she'd really do just that. Maybe Jane would go with her. She fell asleep at last.

Jane woke her an hour or so later when she slid into bed beside her.

Marjorie mumbled, 'God, what time is it? Did you just come to bed?'

'Mmm. I dunno. Two a.m. or something. I drank too much coffee. I'm still wide awake. Do you mind if I talk?'

'Not if you don't mind if I don't open my eyes.' Marjorie's voice was furry.

'I'm still thinking about Gardenvale. I'd like to live there again. It wouldn't be too far out, would it? The streets have got flower names, you know? Gardenia, Magnolia, Lantana . . . I think there was a Primrose Street. I used to love primulas . . .'

'What the heck are primulas?'

'Oh, flowers . . . pale purple, tiny little petals, on a long, thin stem. People used to grow them along their paths.'

'Jesus, Jane, do I have to have a botany lesson at this time of the morning?'

'I *love* primulas. I wonder if people still grow them? Daffodils and hyacinths, you know those little purpley grape hyacinths, gorgeous smell? Lilac. Wisteria. Wisteria, the smell makes me feel drunk.'

Marjorie sat up and blinked heavily at Jane.

'Did you get hold of some pot while I was away?'

Jane said indignantly. '*No!* We decided we didn't need it any more, didn't we? Of course I didn't. I'm just talking.'

Marjorie slid down again and pulled the pillow up around her ears.

'Who did all the weeding?'

'What?'

'Weeding. In your bloody Gardenvale garden.'

'Haven't a clue. I don't remember anyone weeding.'

'Rich bitch. Bet you had a gardener.'

After a few moments, Jane said guiltily, 'We *did* have a gardener. I completely forgot. He came a couple of days a week.'

'I knew it. Middle-class bitch, you even forgot he existed. Typical of the upper classes. Bloody snob.'

'We weren't snobs! Mum used to sit in the kitchen having cups of tea with him and deciding what they'd plant. Now I remember. They used to work in the garden together. We weren't snobs.'

'I bet you had a big date palm in the middle of a buffalo grass lawn.'

'Yes, we did.'

'Snob. What about the back? As if I care.'

'Oh, loganberries, raspberries, blackcurrants. Yum. I used to love those. *Cecil Brunner!*'

Marjorie jumped.

'Don't shout like that. Cecil who?'

'Not who – it. Rose bush. I've been trying to remember its name for years. Lovely pink roses, very tiny, with an exquisite smell. I wonder who he was?'

Marjorie yawned.

'Some pommy freak.' She punched her pillow, went on, 'Listen, I'm going to Melbourne tomorrow. Do you mind if I get some sleep? Thanks for the talk about great gardens of Gardenvale. Goodnight.'

'OK. I'm coming to Melbourne, too, remember? Gotta talk to me Mum. Night.'

Five

Ally had woken feeling afraid. Days were beginning to do their expanding-out-of-sight trick again. In desperation she went to see Fleur, breaking the unspoken rule that usually kept her away from her friend in the early days of one of Fleur's involvements with men.

Fleur answered the door. She looked surprised to see Ally.

'Darling! Hi! You look great. Hang on, no you don't. You look crazy. What's up? Come on in.'

Ally hung back.

'Is it all right?'

'It's all right. Someone you can meet, now you're here.'

Fleur walked swiftly ahead of her, down the carpeted hall to the sun room. She lived high above the road to the peninsula, overlooking the sheltered waters of Port Phillip Bay. Through distant smog the skyscrapers of Melbourne reared like dinosaurs seen through primeval mist.

'You've got a visitor, Fleur?'

'Yep.'

'I won't stay then.'

'Oh, stay, Ally, you might as well. I want you to meet Swain.'

Fleur's hair had been cut short, nipped in at the nape of her slender neck. She was a brunette, with sparkling brown eyes, the whites very white, the brown very deep.

'Did you say Swain, Fleur?'

Fleur lowered her voice.

'S-w-a-i-n, awful, isn't it? His mother was a romantic.'

'What does he do?'

'Ally, you always ask that!'

Ally was talking softly, too.

'Darling, you're a rich divorcee. I'm always scared some man will take advantage of you.'

'Take advantage! You're so old-fashioned. Anyway, he isn't. I haven't had such fun in years.'

59

'Uh-huh.'

'Oh, don't be so cynical. Actually, he's a merchant seaman, but most of all he's a free spirit. We clicked the first time we met. You'll love him.'

Ally doubted that.

'What does he live on, when he's just being a free spirit?'

'You're preparing not to like him, aren't you? Well, he might take off for the other side of the world or he might just stay with me. I don't care. We're having fun. Anyway, I just might go with him. Who cares? We're having a fab time.'

Swain appeared, swaggering down the passage, hair damp and ruffled from the shower. Faded, tight jeans, torso deeply tanned and bare, a shortish, powerfully-built man with bright, sly, cheeky eyes. He looked . . . common . . . and Ally loathed him. 'Common' she'd learned at her mother's knee. Nobody in Gardenvale had to define it. Swain was common and that was it.

Hypocritically, Ally extended a polite hand. Swain squeezed enough to hurt. Something wary was in his eyes as he summed her up, then he set out to charm her. Ally wasn't about to be charmed.

Fleur alarmed her by the casualness with which she took up new men. It frightened Ally, the way she'd invite a new man into her home on short acquaintance.

Swain poured coffee, asked Ally if she wanted more. She said no, thanks, she really had to go.

Fleur said, 'All right, but phone tomorrow, promise?'

Ally nodded. Swain stood with his arm around Fleur as Ally left. He certainly had a great body, with one of those absurd, bulging crotches. What the hell did they stuff in there to make them bulge like that? And how could Fleur fall for someone so unsubtle?

That night Ally sat at the table reading the local free newspaper. A word came into focus. Refuge. That was what she needed. A refuge from life. No! Ally picked up her coffee cup and hurled it across the room. She didn't need a refuge! There was no need for one – she wasn't about to destroy herself again. What if Fleur was busy right now? Good for her. She'd just have to find something to do with herself, couldn't rely on other people. She picked up the paper again, searching for the word that had caught her attention.

A few minutes later, she picked up the phone and dialled a number.

'Oh. Hullo. I've just read in the paper that you need volunteers to work at the refuge. I'd be interested.'

The conversation was brief. She was to go there at about eleven the next morning.

It had been quite simple, after all. A word in a paper catching your eye, a few words over the phone and tomorrow some new experience, so why was she shaking?

Then, feeling foolish, she picked up the phone again.

'Hi, I was just talking to you. Realised I don't know where the refuge is . . . no address in the paper, only the number.'

The voice at the other end of the line sounded friendly and warm. Ally wrote down the address and mysteriously stopped shaking, as though the second call had established a reality of some kind.

In bed she started thinking about it. A women's refuge in Parktown? Parktown was cool, greenish sea, lapping on to gritty sand, destination of childhood Sunday drives, picnics on prickly grass beneath ti-trees. It was holiday homes, retired couples. Wasn't it? Huge, rich mansions hidden away on the cliffs, rickety wooden steps zig-zagging steeply to private beaches. It was Melbourne Cup day picnics, going to the end of the line on the train, little kids with buckets and spades. A women's refuge in Parktown?

Next morning, where the road curved round the great red bluff, she pulled off into the look-out parking area and saw to her surprise that Parktown sprawled far and wide. How could she not have noticed? She'd read about factories locating there, decentralised, knew of the industrial strip, but how come she hadn't realised the whole atmosphere of the place had changed?

She found the street she wanted, slowed as she searched for the number and drove past when she found it. Round the block, past it, speeding up again.

Women's refuge. Oh lord, militant feminists, like Marjorie? Lesbians, maybe, she thought timidly. Clever women, anyway, educated. Women like you saw on the idiot box, waving banners, shoving policemen, shouting, laughing. And Ally ageing, privileged, soft, ill-educated. Nervous as hell. What was she going to do? Sit in her car? Too scared to give it a go?

It was a big, old, timber house, rather like that she'd lived in as a child in Gardenvale. Set well back from the road behind a buffalo grass lawn with tall trees around the edge. By the front door a shabby pram. She walked up the path slowly. Beside the pram, an old thong, one little sandal, a discarded wet nappy hanging, pins still in it, holding the shape of a small bottom.

She rang the bell. The solid, timber door opened, and, dimly seen through the mesh of the security door, a woman smiled.

'Hi. Come in. You're Ally?'

She nodded.

'I'm Sylvia.'

Ally followed her to a big room with a bay window.

'Sit down, will you? Won't be a moment.'

She picked up a packet of tampons, 'Just have to give these to one of the ladies.'

The desk was cluttered with books and papers, cardboard folders, three empty coffee mugs, two teaspoons that had dripped on to papers, a jar of pencils and ballpoint pens, scraps of paper jammed in with them, a telephone, more pieces of paper scribbled on, three partly-chewed jelly beans, a packet of sultanas. Posters on the walls, newspaper clippings and meeting notices and agendas pinned to a board. In one corner a single bed, made up, an Indian quilt draped over it. Cupboards lined one wall. Through one open door she saw canned foods, cereal, flour, sugar, coffee, tea, canister of biscuits.

The phone rang. Ally jumped. It kept ringing. Uncertainly, she picked it up. Before she could speak, a tiny voice came to her ears, 'That the refuge?'

'Yes.'

'Can you come and get me?'

'Hold on for a moment, please.'

'*No!* Don't go away. Just come and get me. I'm in *trouble*! Listen, the address . . .'

'I'll just go and get . . .'

'Jesus, will you just write the address down? I'm at sixteen . . .'

In the background, an incredibly loud noise and someone shouting, a scream, a crash, a loud male voice, 'Bugger off!' and at the other end of the line the receiver crashed down. To its death, by the sound of it.

Sylvia came back.

'Thanks for answering the phone. Nothing important?'

'I think it was. I'm awfully sorry, I messed it up. Some woman needing help and I didn't get the address in time. A man yelled at me and slammed the phone down.'

'Don't worry about it. She'll call again. Sorry you copped that the first time you answered the phone.'

Guiltily, Ally noticed the appearance of two vertical lines between Sylvia's eyebrows.

'I'll do better next time.'

Sylvia smiled: 'Of course you will.'

She made coffee in the tiny kitchen off the office and brought out two cups. Beyond the kitchen was a cramped bathroom, with shower, wash basin and toilet. Sylvia showed it to her.

'For staff and volunteers only. Saves us getting worms and infections.'

Ally was shocked and must have looked apprehensive. Sylvia grinned.

'Well, we like to think it does, anyway.'

She was quite tall and slender, with long, brown hair, hazel eyes and a tanned complexion. She wore an olive-green wrap-around skirt, unfashionably long, a heavy shapeless sweater and flat, canvas, strap shoes. Sylvia looked nothing at all like a militant feminist.

'So, tell me, Ally, why do you want to do volunteer work at a refuge?'

'I'm not sure I'm suitable. I think maybe I'm wasting your time.'

'You must have been interested to ring last night.'

'Oh, I'm interested all right. I just don't feel, well, qualified and capable, now I'm here.'

'Normal reaction. Everyone feels like that at first. I'm sure you could handle things. It's not all crisis and drama. Lots of ordinary things, like washing bedclothes and cleaning up when kids are sick, taking kids to the doctor, just talking to women and reassuring them, helping them wash up and clean the place. Bit of letter writing and book work and all that. Anyone can do it. We do need more people to help. Not many turn up. I half thought you wouldn't. I'm really glad you came. Well, what do you think?'

'I'd like to try. Is there any training I have to do?'

'On the job, mostly. It's not something you can teach anyone. Might do a few workshops later on when you see how you like it and we see how we like you.'

Sylvia went on: 'Later on, if you stay, we'll be looking at more paid staff. We're fighting for more funding. Just scraping by at the moment with only a few paid workers. You'd have to be a volunteer until we screw more money out of the government.'

Ally nodded. 'That's OK. I mean, I'd like a paid job when you can afford it, but I'm OK to do volunteer work if that's the way it is.'

'Yes, well, the only real qualification is that you do care about other women, to the point where you don't judge them or lay your own standards on them and you don't categorise them or patronise them. You learn everything else on the job, legal rights, social security rights, all that stuff.'

Sylvia smiled at her.

63

'It's a burn-out job, Ally, but you'll know when it's time to go. I thought I had heart trouble a while back, getting this pain in my heart, as though something was sticking into it. Then I realised I only got it when I was sitting listening to what some woman had lived through, never when I was rushing around.'

She stood up briskly and picked up the coffee cups.

'Would it be too much to ask you to stay on now? I'm short of staff. One had to go away in a hurry. Her old man found out where she was working and he's violent. She buzzed off to work in a Sydney refuge. Oh yes, not just the residents who've got hassles. Nearly everyone here has got problems. All in it together, I guess.'

The phone rang and Ally jumped again. She'd have to stop doing that. Sylvia spoke briefly and hung up.

'Well, can you stay?'

'Yes. That's fine. What do I do first?'

'Write your name and address and phone number in this book. By the way, we use first names only to the residents, the cops and anyone else. Don't ever disclose anything about any of the workers or the residents to *anyone*, OK? Very important.'

The door bell chimed and Sylvia went to answer it. The phone rang again and somewhere in the house someone screamed. Sylvia reappeared, 'Ally, you can answer that, will you?'

Ally wrote down the message from a government department. The woman was still screaming. She hurried out of the office and almost collided with Sylvia, who was leading in a woman whose nose was red and swollen beneath a blackened eye.

Sylvia took the sleeping child from the woman's arms and handed her gently to Ally.

'Don't panic about the screaming. It'll be a woman called Winnie. On your way to Winnie, put this little one into an empty bed you'll find in the first room on the right, down the passage, OK? Take it easy now.'

The child was breathing heavily. She was pale and dirty and smelly. Ally held her tightly. On the child's face was the pink imprint of a large hand. Around her neck were scratches and dried blood. Ally tucked the child into the bed, sat there watching her, thinking of Jane.

The screaming had stopped and somewhere someone was crying.

The bedroom she went to next was at the end of a long passage, near a door with stained glass panels. A woman was crouched on a bed, rocking back and forth, two other women beside her.

In a voice of mild irritation, one said, 'Jesus, where've you *been*? I thought one of youse'd never come. You're new, aren't you? I'm Mercy, this is Elsa and this here making all the noise is Winnie. Winnie, shut up, someone's here now. What's your name? I'm going to make some tea. Want some?'

Ally shook her head. 'No, thanks, I just had coffee. I'm Ally.'

'I'll get some for them, then.'

Elsa stood and stretched. 'I'm going with Mercy. Can you manage with Winnie?'

Ally nodded, sitting on the bed, never having felt less adequate.

'Sylvia tell you, you won't get anywhere with Winnie? She's as nutty as a fruit cake; psych case, dunno why they have her here.'

From the doorway Mercy said, 'Because she's got nowhere else to go, dummy.'

Ally found a bathroom and searched in a linen cupboard for a flannel. She rinsed it out and went back to the still-crying Winnie. She squatted beside her, raised her face gently, patted the blotched skin with the cool cloth. A hand frail as a bird's claw reached out to her. Winnie's eyes were red around the edges; her nose was scaly. She had thin, greying hair and her breath was foul. Ally's stomach cramped tight, as though encased in an old-fashioned corset. Winnie put both arms around her, clung tightly.

'You're kind. I don't know what I'd do without youse. You're kind.'

Squirming across the bed, she said, 'I'm going to sleep.'

Curled foetus-like, face to the wall, she closed her eyes and seemed instantly to sleep. Ally drew a blanket over her, tucked it in, and smoothed the straggling hair. As she went down the passage the door bell chimed. The office door was closed. Ally opened the front door. Beyond the locked security door stood a man. Automatically, Ally started to turn the key to open the door. From beside her, out of sight from the man, a hand flashed out and gripped hers and a voice hissed, 'Don't open it! Can't you see it's a man?'

The hand let hers go and Ally left the key untouched.

'Can I help you?' she asked instead.

A stream of foul language swamped her, tucked within it the message that he wanted someone called Norma and if he didn't see her he was going to tear the fucking refuge apart. Mercy whispered from beside her, 'Tell him to get lost. Say she's not here. Say you'll get the pigs.'

In a shaky voice, Ally said loudly, 'I'm sorry, I can't divulge that information and if you don't leave I'm afraid I'll have to call the police to remove you.'

Ally's voice seemed to send him berserk. A huge fist began battering at the mesh of the door.

'Shut it! Shut it!'

Ally slammed the wooden door and Mercy beside her was convulsed with mirth. Ally glared at her.

'Why are you laughing like that? It's not funny. I was scared sick.'

'It's the way you talked to him. So ladylike. It sounded funny.'

Over the thunderous hammering from outside, Ally raised her voice and said loudly, 'Well, give me time. I'm only new. I'll learn.'

Mercy laughed and hugged her. Sylvia came out from the office.

'Everything OK, Ally? Was that a big chap asking for Norma?'

Mercy said, 'Yeah, and you'd better call the pigs. Listen to him. He's not kidding.'

Sylvia sighed and returned to the office. Like a ghost, Winnie appeared, carving knife grasped in upraised fist. Ally quickly went to her, gently took the knife.

'Winnie, it's all right. Everything's all right. Go back to bed.'

Winnie turned and wandered away, muttering to herself. Ally's stomach had gone loose. It went through her mind that she was having a very physical day. Mercy walked down the passage carrying a thick slice of bread and something. Elsa called after her, 'Don't you feed the damned cockroaches with that, Merce. You're not supposed to eat in our room.'

Without turning, Mercy jabbed two fingers in the air.

In the office, Sylvia put down the phone.

Norma lay on her side of the bed.

'I don't know how he found me so quick. Someone must have told him I was coming here. Probably the cabbie.'

'Well, the police'll be here in a minute.'

'Do they always come at once?' Ally asked.

'Usually. Depends who you talk to. Most of them hate "domestics" and they know we take a lot they'd have to handle if we weren't here, so it pays them to give us protection.'

In the distance a siren was wailing. There was a final violent assault on the door, then the sound of heavy feet on the path, receding, followed by a metallic crash.

'Now what was that?' Sylvia frowned. 'Oh, shit, did you leave your car out front, Ally? I meant to tell you to put it round the back. We can lock the back gate and they're pretty secure there. We'll pay for the panel beating, bring the bill to the office. Don't forget now.'

The police arrived. Sylvia went out and spoke to them. When she came back, she said, 'He got away, of course. God knows why they have to switch their damned siren on like that. Honest, I think they try to warn them. Norma, I'm going to take you up to the hospital now. Can you manage, Ally?'

'Yes, I'm fine.'

'Like me to bring you back something for lunch? Make yourself tea or coffee, if you want.'

Norma muttered, 'I'm sorry to be a nuisance.'

Sylvia put an arm around her.

'Who said you were a nuisance, dopey? What do you think we're here for? Come on, let's go.'

It was after five o'clock that afternoon when Ally went home. She'd met two more staff workers, Joan and Yvette, talked with more of the women who were living in the house, and had been run off her feet. She drove away in her dented car, drained of energy, head throbbing with painful tension. No way was she going to work at that madhouse. Nobody could be expected to work like that, day after day.

Next day, she decided to take her car to the panel beater and do some shopping while she waited for it. It upset her to see that evidence of violence. She'd leave the car and walk around to the refuge and explain to them that she couldn't work there after all. If the security door hadn't been locked he could have beaten her up. She remembered the marks and scratches on Norma's daughter, little Gayleen. What kind of man would hit his own child? Ally decided she wouldn't even go in to Parktown.

She went back into the house and stood at the window, listening to the ocean's endless roar. She opened a door to let the salt wind in. Before she'd left the refuge, Joan had said to her, almost absentmindedly, 'Ally, just check to see nobody follows you home. That drongo of a bloke might be hanging around. He probably wouldn't follow you, but don't take any chances. If you're suspicious any time, drive to the police station.'

Naturally she'd been paranoiac on the way home, especially driving down the long dirt road to her house, trees overhanging each side. Insane even to consider working at a place that could send you batty the first day. The place had a smell, too, and some of the women, like Winnie, weren't even clean.

It was cosy in her house. She closed the door again. Quiet, too. Lonely. Boring.

She went back. Sylvia looked up when she walked in.

'Hi, had a feeling you mightn't show up again. You struck quite a day yesterday. Not always like that.'

'It did cross my mind, who needs a job like this? I did think, who wants that kind of trouble in their life? Next thing, I was here.'

Sylvia said mildly, 'Yes, we've noticed that dementia is transmitted amazingly fast in this place.'

As time had once slowed down, now it speeded up amazingly. Ally didn't go to the refuge every day, but there was always something to do. She knew more people now, went to meetings, a film night, a lecture. One afternoon when she got home from the refuge she heard the phone ringing and ran for the door, key ready. It would be Jane, she thought. It wasn't. It was Rowley, calling from the other side of the world.

'Rowley? Where are you?'

'I'm still in London. Ally, there's something I have to tell you. Verna and I were in a car accident . . .'

'Are you all right, Rowley?'

'A few bruises, a cut or two, nothing much. It's Verna. She was badly hurt. Internal injuries.'

'I'm so sorry.'

'Ally, she died.'

Ally's mind went blank.

'Ally, are you still there?'

'Yes.'

'I just thought you should know. I'm coming home again. I had the funeral yesterday. It's what Verna's family suggested, have it over here. Too much, that business of getting her home. So sad to do that . . . everyone waiting around for the funeral. It was best to do it here.'

'Yes.'

Verna dead? That perfection . . . decaying . . . Did he mean coming home to Australia or coming home to his wife?

'I feel really bad, Ally.'

'I understand.'

'About everything, Ally. Putting you through all that. I saw what it did to you. I had no idea all that would happen . . . the morning up on the headland, the night at the beach house. It's like a nightmare. Bringing Verna over here, to die.'

'You can't blame yourself for the accident.'

Rowley's voice was so far away . . .

'Ally? It didn't work out with Verna. We both made a mistake, we'd realised that. It wasn't working at all. I'd decided to come home, even before the accident. We'd been talking about it, that day. It was a relief to both of us, to decide it'd be better if we split up.'

Please shut up, Rowley, she was thinking, I don't want to know about it. And, aloud, 'When are you flying out?'

'I'm not sure. A week or so. I'll phone again when I've booked.'

So soon. Ally stared at the wall where two paintings hung awry as they never had when Rowley was around.

'Is there anything I can do to help?'

'Thanks for offering, Ally. Not really. Wait a minute, could you ring some of Verna's friends and tell them . . . I can give you phone numbers.'

'No! No, I can't do that.'

'Sorry. I shouldn't have asked.'

'Rowley, take care. I have to go. Goodbye. I'm sorry.'

She put the phone down gently and sat staring blankly at the wall. Verna dead. She was glad now that she'd never had bitter or hateful feelings towards the other woman. When the feeling of shock began to abate, Ally discovered another rising in her mind. What was it? She was an astronaut left on the launching pad, flight aborted . . . a little girl off to a party, told the birthday kid had measles and the party was cancelled. She walked into the hall where the tall vase had once stood, thought of Rowley's scratched and dented trophies boxed in the garage, a collection of junk.

It bothered her all that night and in her dreams she staggered over an endless plain bearing the vase in her arms, endlessly tumbling over trophies, embedded like golf tees before her. Next morning she gathered all the things she'd destroyed and damaged – so long ago, in another life, surely – and put them into green garbage bags and drove to the council rubbish dump. A grader was pushing dirt over levelled rubbish. She drove as close to it as she could. A man strode towards her from a small hut; she guessed him to be the official scavenger-caretaker, constantly on the alert lest a member of the unscrupulous, law-despising public deprive him of his rights. Ally grasped her bags, clambered awkwardly over piles of rubbish and tossed them one by one towards the great all-concealer, the moving blade of the dozer. They landed short, with an interesting clatter and chink.

'What's wrong with you, lady?' The voice was loud and angry and came from behind. 'Can't you bloody read? I got a notice there says dump your rubbish *there*, not where you flung it. You drove right past it. I seen you.'

'What difference does it make? It's only three damned bags, not a truckload.'

Wobbling on the smelly rubbish, dignity lost, Ally became aggressive. She plunged back to her car. When she glanced back, the wretched fellow was heading for the green garbage bags that had made such interesting sounds. She screamed at him, 'That's mine! Leave it alone!'

Ignoring her, he kept going. Ally went after him, legs sinking again into the disgusting mess. He reached her bags and went past without a glance.

Teetering, she turned and squelched back again, gasping for breath. It was heavy stuff to walk in. Sliding behind the wheel, she saw that the man had now turned and had hefted one of her bags in his hand. Defeated, she thrust her head from the window and screeched, 'What *are* you? Big fucking *brother*?'

Hah! Didn't have any trouble saying it that time, did she? Ally slammed into reverse, wheels spinning, heard a blasting horn, braked hard and looked over her shoulder at an elderly couple, regarding her open-mouthed and enraged from the sudden insecurity of their car, menaced by hers. They, too, she saw happily, had driven past the damned notice. Let the Lunatic-in-Residence turn his wrath on them. Let him read poor Rowley's name on the battered trophies. Why should she care?

Exhausted, she drove away, went home and had a long shower to clean the muck from her legs and the smell from her hair.

At the refuge there was a woman in the office with lower lip split and swollen like a small party frankfurter that had been left overlong in boiling water.

Sylvia said, 'Ally, this is Roxanne. Ally will look after you, Roxanne. You go out to the kitchen and put the jug on. Ally'll be out in a minute.'

To Ally she said wearily, 'I've been here all night. It's been bedlam. I haven't filled in a form for Roxanne, can you do that? I've got to get home and have a few hours sleep. I've had it. You be OK?' She focused on Ally, 'Hey, are you all right?'

'Oh, sure. Just a few little problems.'

'Want to talk?'

'Some time, maybe.'

'Yes, well. Don't forget, we got rights too.'

Ally smiled, 'I won't forget.'

'I'm off now. Ring Yvette if things get too hectic. She went off at five, so she'll have had a few hours sleep.'

Ally went to the kitchen. Roxanne was sipping her tea painfully.

Women and kids were coming and going, some cooking; a radio was turned up loudly, a small boy came hurtling down the passage on a tricycle and Ally moved swiftly.

'Take that outside, sweetie. No riding in here. You might break someone's leg.'

Obediently, the boy pedalled away. Roxanne put her cup down and unbuttoned her blouse, looking up at Ally. She pulled the material aside to disclose a breast shockingly bruised. Silence descended. The women all stared. Ally's stomach curdled.

'Lucky he only punched me. He reckoned he was going to cut my nipple off, only he couldn't find any sharp knives. Lucky, I'd hidden them.'

One of the women said sharply, 'Yes, OK, but cover up, will you? I don't want my kids to see that. Their dreams are bad enough now.'

Roxanne pulled her blouse closed.

'The cops got him anyway. I told Sylvia, I'm gunna charge him this time. She said I could do that and today I'm going to another refuge, so he can't find me when they let him out.'

Ally took Roxanne into the office. Roxanne lay quietly on the bed while Ally filled in the form and then read the daybook, the shabby book with pages dog-eared from rapid turning, that linked each worker like a lifeline.

A man had rung repeatedly during the night, she read, very abusive and violent. Neither Sylvia nor Yvette had recognised the voice. He said he was coming to the refuge to smash it up with his axe.

Nervously, Ally checked that the security door was locked, took the key out and hung it on the high hook, put her head around the kitchen door and said, 'Be sure nobody answers the front door but me, all right?'

In the afternoon the house overflowed with women and children. It was the fortnightly meeting day for residents, ex-residents, workers. Everyone sat in a big room. The air was blue with cigarette smoke. Ally kept going back to the office to answer the phone. Sylvia came back in, smiled, 'Don't let it throw you, Ally. Everyone feels like bolting for the first few weeks, especially on meeting day. If you're still here in three months, you'll think you've got used to it and it won't be that, you'll have just gone psycho, like the rest of us.'

The phone kept ringing, babies cried, children grizzled and fought, voices droned on, women laughed, women cried, women argued, turned to hug, moved away from each other, came back and hugged, half laughing, half crying. The most trivial incidents seemed to take for ever to thrash out. Ally's head was throbbing. When it was over, someone she hadn't met came over to her, 'Hi, you're Ally, aren't you? I'm Lynsey. I've been on holiday. Want to come up town and have a coffee with me?'

'Yes, please!'

The two women sat by the window, in a small café overlooking the bay. Lynsey ordered cream cakes.

Lynsey looked to be a little older than Ally, with a silky, grey cluster of curls, cut short. Her eyes were large and grey – unusual eyes, not often you saw grey with no blue mixed in. She had a slim figure and wore jeans and a roll-neck sweater. Her face was quite lined, her skin clear and flawless.

'The only time I eat cake is after those terrible meetings we're committed to. Incredible, aren't they? Everyone gets a blinding headache and we never seem to get anywhere.'

'Why do we have them, then?'

'Gives everyone a chance to clear the shit off their liver, have a say in what happens at the place.' She stirred her coffee. 'Messy place to work, isn't it? I keep asking myself why I'm here, all that drama and confusion, who needs it? It makes you overreact. Funny sometimes. Someone comes in, terrified of her bloke and he builds up in your mind until you have this image of a guy as big as a Harlem Globetrotter and half the time when he turns up, you open the door and here's this little guy standing there, you think you could knock over with one finger.'

Ally said, 'I was thinking in bed about it the other night, how weird it is. There we are in that nice old house in a nice old early-Parktown street, neighbours going about their business each side and at our place we're a little community under siege, you know? I thought what we see and hear there only happened in really bad, underprivileged areas.'

Lynsey told her how she used to live in Heidelberg as a kid and going to Parktown was a big event, a day at the beach.

'I always dreamed of living here, so when my old man died I came here, like coming to a retirement village. And then the place exploded with supermarkets and subdivisions and shopping complexes and bowling alleys and water slides, the whole crazy eighties thing.'

'How did you get involved with the refuge?'

'Accidentally. A nice little family moved in next door and every Friday night he used to come home drunk and beat them all up. I got so upset I went and had a talk to the cops and they suggested I tell the woman about the refuge, so I did and we both went in and had a talk and I just got interested. It seemed a useful thing to be doing.'

'Did she come in to the refuge? Your neighbour?'

'No, she didn't. They moved away.'

Ally said, 'I'm going to have more coffee, do you want some, too?'

'Ally, do you live alone?'

'At the moment.'

Lynsey raised her eyebrows.

'Well, my husband left me for another woman and now he says he's coming back. I'm not sure if he means just coming back to the country – he's overseas – or back to me. She died, killed in a car crash, his – uh – lady.'

'I don't know about you, Ally, but it's only in the last few years I've found out I can live alone with great success. I went from my parents' home into my first marriage, had three kids, got divorced, married again, both times picked men who drank just a bit too much. Not alcoholics, just good old Aussie drinkers. I stayed with the second because I didn't know what else to do. Scared of being alone. Kids all grew up, finished up hundreds of miles from me. When I was widowed, I was almost paralytic with fright. Took me two years to discover I was deliriously happy all day by my little old self. I wouldn't get hitched again if you offered me a million dollars. You know what bothers me now? Thinking of what I laid on my two husbands, insisting they were responsible for my happiness.'

'I know! I know! Putting that on a man, making him responsible for your happiness . . . why do we do that?'

'Brainwashed, I guess.'

Ally stirred her coffee.

'Lynsey, why are so many marriages breaking down? I was looking through the card index at the refuge and *hundreds* of women and kids are passing through this one. It's unbelievable!'

'Well, I guess they're not all broken marriages, there's the psych cases and the homeless women and the girls who can't get jobs, but have you noticed most of them are related to alcohol? You'll find a lot of women say, "He's such a beautiful man when he's sober and I'm terrified of him when he's drunk . . ." I guess that's why I stayed with my old bugger until he died . . . the beautiful bit when he was sober.'

'Do you live on your own, Lynsey?'

'I did until I came to work at the refuge. Now Heather shares with me. We get on really well.'

'I was lucky with Rowley, my husband. Alcohol was never a problem. I wonder now if I wasn't a big bore. I depended on him for everything.' She smiled at the other woman. 'It's fantastic to have

other women to talk to. My problem is, I'm not sure I want Rowley to
come back to me. I've changed so much. I'm really not the same wife he
remembers from just a few months ago. It scares me a bit, as though
I've gone out of control. Really strange things are happening to me.
My life gone haywire!'

Lynsey laughed heartily.

'It's known as living, Ally! Gets to be a habit. It's what happens
when you break out and get into it, every day, every minute, making
the most of it, good, bad or indifferent.'

Driving home that day, thinking of Rowley, certain things about
living with Rowley that were warm and comforting. Going home now
to a silent and dark house. But she was used to that. Perhaps if he came
back, things'd be different this time. How would he react to her
working? At a refuge, of all places? And the changes in her, the feeling
that she was growing – she couldn't let that come to a stop. Why should
she have Rowley back again? So it didn't work out and poor Verna
died. It was Rowley's problem, not hers.

The days went by quickly. She kept meaning to get in touch with
Jane, to phone or write, but somehow didn't get around to it. She'd
become a permanent volunteer and was sent to do a course in working
with women in crisis. She discovered you weren't supposed to just sit
there with them like a blob, nor tell them to pull up their socks and not
to worry because everything would turn out fine, rather you had to
concentrate on reflecting back to them what they were saying, not
letting your thoughts slide defensively away from the tragedy of their
lives or the grotty mess they were, to what you might have for dinner
that night and whether the skirt you'd just bought was too tight and the
wrong colour.

It scared her because she could see if you didn't do it right, you'd
make things worse for them. And if you *did* do it right, they'd come
apart at the seams right in front of you, tell you things you weren't
really wanting to hear.

Chopping vegetables for her dinner, Ally stared at an onion,
reflected that people were like onions, unpeeled like them. She looked
with watering eyes at the way the onion was constructed in layers that
separated once you broke in. Right in the middle was the tiny core,
pure and whole and still capable of making you cry. She was entranced
by the analogy, talked to Heather about it the next day.

'It scares me a bit, Heather, because the more I listen to other
women, the looser I feel, as though I'm starting to fall apart too.'

Heather said thoughtfully, that it was a normal reaction

when you began working at the refuge.

'When I met you first, Ally, you were quite uptight, weren't you? It's a two-way exchange, in a way, when you're talking to women in crisis. A lot of what they say, what they've experienced, keys in to your own life, doesn't it?'

Ally nodded uncertainly.

'I suppose so. I get really nervous when they start to talk. Scared of what I'm going to hear.'

'I know. You just have to relax and use things you're learning all the time, skills you've learned from your own life. You've got them, you know Ally, or you wouldn't be here.'

'I have?'

'Of course. All you need to do, whatever a woman is telling you, is feed it back to her, keep feeding back so she can keep talking, getting it out into the open.'

'I'm not used to people being so, so reliant on me.'

'Well, the woman who's in the crisis that brought her here, she's the one who's doing all the work, you just take it easy. She's doing the agonising, not you. You can't do a thing to help until she realises there's something in her life she wants to change. No pushing for information, just relax and reflect back what she's telling you, see? Don't worry anyway, you're doing great, Ally.'

Ally was being encouraged to take more responsibility at the refuge. Now when a woman came to the door, it was sometimes Ally who conducted the vital first interview. She'd learned early not to put a desk between them but to sit close by, ready to put out a comforting or reassuring hand, never to set up the classic client-counsellor situation. That wasn't what the refuge was about.

The worst thing she had to endure was cigarette smoke. Ally had never been a smoker and once Rowley gave it up she'd become used to a smoke-free environment. Now her hair and her clothes were impregnated by it. Ally hated it. Her eyes watered, her nose and throat became over-sensitive to it. Yet how could she say to some trembling, distressed woman, 'Please don't smoke while you're talking to me'? It simply couldn't be done, so she put up with it, knowing that what she was engaged in at the refuge was so important, personal discomfort must be overlooked. Sometimes she felt indignant about it, felt like blurting out to the others, 'Hey, isn't this part of being exploited by society, all these women smoking like mad? Why don't we do something about it?' but didn't feel confident enough yet to be so outspoken, especially when most of the workers smoked heavily themselves.

Six

Jane hadn't driven around Gardenvale in years. She was afraid it would have changed almost beyond recognition, as so many other places did when you saw them again after a lapse of time. The changes she saw were good ones. It was in places like this near-beach suburb, she reflected, that the greening of the metropolis had begun, in shade trees planted in suburban gardens, in the growing love for native trees and native shrubs once spurned in favour of exotic plants from other countries. She'd been searching for a flat, and instead came home with the key to a house. Marjorie had just arrived in their room in a cheap guesthouse and had take-away dinners in the oven. She was bubbling with excitement, too, after a stimulating day. Jane interrupted her after a while.

'That's really great, Marjorie. Sounds as though the health service is going to be a goer, but listen, I've found the perfect place for us. I was scared someone else would grab it, so I've paid the bond money and all that and, we've got an option to buy, too, if we can swing it and if you love it as much as I do. I can't wait for you to see it.'

Marjorie looked a little irritated.

'Hang on, aren't you moving a bit fast? Shouldn't I have had the chance to be in on the decision, too?'

'Look, I'm in a hurry to settle down somewhere, Marjorie. I know you'll love it.'

'Primulas down the path, has it got?'

'As a matter of fact, it has.'

Marjorie grinned and ruffled Jane's hair.

'OK. Let's gobble down this ghastly food and give ourselves indigestion and then we'll go and look at it.'

The house was tucked away in a quiet street that finished in a park, where ancient willows slumped over a rather muddy-looking lake. There was a large garden around the house. Marjorie murmured appreciatively, 'It's quite a gem, Janey. Federation style, eh? I thought you'd gone clucky again,' Jane felt herself blushing, 'but I see what you mean. It'd be quite a good investment if we could raise the money. OK. Let's look inside.'

It was larger than she'd expected, three good-sized bedrooms and a sleep-out, a rambling, high-ceilinged place, with wide passages and an entrance hall and a huge old kitchen that would give them plenty of exercise walking from stove to fridge to sink. Marjorie said dubiously, 'It's awfully big. Are you sure it wouldn't be too much damned work, looking after it? I'm not into domesticity, you know, I never promised you that.'

Jane said, with a nervous clearing of her throat, 'Well, there's something I have to tell you, Marjorie.'

Marjorie sat quietly while Jane told her of Ben's visit. Jane couldn't tell what she was feeling and said nervously, 'I'm not sure, but it's starting to look as though I could be pregnant again. My breasts are feeling sensitive and they look kind of blue-veiney.' Hurriedly she went on, 'Hey, I'm not going into my phantom baby bit again, honest. I'd like to know what you're thinking, Marjorie. It was your idea, after all.'

Through the uncurtained windows of the room in which they were talking, a last flood of deep golden sunshine had placed a halo of brilliant light around Marjorie's head as she sat on the carpeted floor. Motes danced, spun, flew upwards and downwards in a shimmering cloud. Marjorie was looking up at Jane, still silent. Jane said nervously, 'God, this place is dusty. If we take it, we'll have to get the carpet shampoo-ed before we move any furniture in.'

Marjorie stood, stretched, still made no comment.

'Marjorie! Don't give me the silent treatment. What's wrong with you?'

'Nothing's wrong. Well, it's like this; my brain is full of what I've been doing today. I could handle the new house bit, and I was feeling fine about it, feeling everything was happening in an organised, orderly, sensible way and I was looking ahead at a completely different scene than you were, Jane. I thought you'd stopped being . . . tricky. I mean, how could you keep from me what happened while I was away? It makes me feel really unsure of you.'

Jane said, 'Now wait a minute . . .'

'Hang on, I haven't finished. You asked me to talk, OK? When I came back from Murwillumbah, it was fantastic to find you on top of everything again, over your depression, full of energy, planning the future. You seemed to have got it all together so well. And now you're telling me about this guy and that makes me feel strange, because it wasn't work you did on yourself that snapped you out of the low, it was fucking this guy. That makes me feel insecure, Jane.'

Uncomfortably, Jane said, 'I felt funny when you got back, Marjorie . . .'

Marjorie interrupted, 'It makes me wonder . . . Look, if you didn't think you were pregnant, would you have told me about him?'

'His name's Ben, why can't you say his name? Of course I'd have told you. Oh, shit, maybe I wouldn't. What would have been the point? Does it matter now?'

'Yes, it does matter. How come he could sort you out when I couldn't?'

'Because . . .'

'You enjoyed it, didn't you?'

Jane's face turned ruddy in the warm light. She nodded her head guiltily, said quickly, 'In a fun sort of way, that's all. Oh, all right, I enjoyed it more than that. I let myself go with it, because I had the feeling that if I didn't, I wouldn't get pregnant, you know? And if I got pregnant, I wanted it to be by someone I really liked. It wouldn't have seemed fair to the baby, otherwise. Marjorie, I thought you'd be pleased.'

Marjorie sighed suddenly. 'It's OK.' She reached out and pulled Jane close. 'Look, it's all right. It's done now. It's going to be fine. It's what we both wanted, isn't it? You just made me feel funny, making decisions that affect our future, screwing a guy I've never seen and not telling me straight away.'

Jane said humbly, 'I felt nervous. I'm sorry.'

Jane felt a little strange. What had just happened between them had been very . . . married . . . almost as though Marjorie was a husband who'd had unwelcome news of an unplanned pregnancy. She said, 'When the baby's one or two, I was thinking I could get a job. If I worked somewhere between here and Parktown, Mum would probably love to look after the baby. Maybe a part-time job until it's ready to go to school.'

'Got some explaining to do to Ally before then though, haven't you?'

'I know. I'm going to see her this week. I'll talk to her about us, then later on, I can tell her about the baby.'

Marjorie was staring at her.

'God, you really are such a devious little bitch, Jane. You amaze me. You're such a good counsellor with other people, and yet with yourself, in your own life, you dodge and squirm like a rabbit. Oh, don't look like that! I think it's funny. I'm not being heavy. You're a nut! Listen, darling, it won't be so bad, talking to Ally. She knows about us. She's known for a long time. You're just winkling it out into the open. It'll be a relief to her.'

Jane kept putting off phoning Ally. Things were happening so quickly and she was busy renovating the house. When the phone was connected, she ran out of excuses. When Marjorie came home that night, Jane was looking stunned.

'You'd better sit down before I tell you this bit of news. I rang Mum . . .'

'Oh, great. I was beginning to think you'd chickened out completely. How did she take it?'

'She didn't. I mean, I didn't tell her. She got in with her news first. She's got herself a job.'

'So? That's great, but so what?'

'So what? She's working at Parktown refuge, that's what's so what!'

Jane had never before seen Marjorie so totally surprised. She gaped at Jane comically. Jane started to laugh.

'The look on your face, Marjorie. That's how I must have looked when Mum told me.'

After the two women had talked it over for a while, Marjorie said, 'You know, this's going to make it just that little bit easier for Ally to accept the way things are, with us and the baby and all. She's jumped out of her little ivory tower and she's not just living in the real world at last, she's having her nose rubbed in it.'

Later, Jane said curiously, 'Marjorie, how did your mother take it, when you told her you were a lesbian. You never actually got around to telling me about that.'

'Fairly standard reaction. Thought it was her fault because she'd never provided me with a father figure. Went on a guilt trip. Thought I was in for a lifetime of being hurt and rejected by society.'

Jane waited expectantly.

'Well, go on. Did she get around to feeling all right about it?'

'She seemed to. I'm not quite sure. I was surprised she took it like that. She'd always been this wonderful role-model to me.' Marjorie shook her head doubtfully. 'Oh, well, maybe it was a bad time to tell her. I was still floundering a bit then, kept coming home with different friends I had a crush on and Mum was stuck for a while on the myth that all homosexuals are out to seduce their own sex all the time. Half the time she looked scared out of her wits.'

Jane said, 'I'm not looking forward to telling Mum and you're not making it any better.'

'You know, I've never been quite sure I wasn't the reason she suddenly married Lance and pissed off to the US. I'm going to fly over some time and check that out. Besides, I miss her. Maybe the three of us can go. Be fun, wouldn't it?'

'The three of us?'

'You, me, the baby?'

'Oh, yes, the *baby*.' She smiled broadly. 'That sounds terrific, doesn't it, making plans for the baby already. You really don't mind, then?'

Marjorie said, 'It was a bit of a shock at first, but I'm happy about it now. Janey, I went off to Murwillumbah feeling guilty about leaving you because you were so down and I just didn't seem to be helping you and when I came back, you were floating around on some kind of a private cloud. Then when you told me what happened while I was away, I felt kind of funny, because it seemed as though he'd done what I couldn't. I don't just mean a baby, I mean the whole bit... you feeling so great.'

'Well, it's just that you were right all along, Marjorie. I needed a baby. Simple as that.' It made Jane feel embarrassed to talk about Ben and she went on quickly, 'Does your stepfather know? About the lesbian thing?'

'I don't know. I didn't tell him. I don't know if Mum did or not. I certainly didn't feel it was any of his business. He was such a nice sort of guy and I didn't want to risk wrecking Mum's romance. Some men get threatened, you know, take it as though it's a personal insult to their manhood. The superiority bit. If you prefer another woman you're saying you don't need a man and some get funny about that, want to prove to you that you're wrong. Not that Lance would have been like that.'

'Your mother doesn't write to you much.'

'That's nothing. I don't think I ever saw her write a letter in my life.'

Marjorie got up and selected a cassette, slid it into the hi-fi. Over the opening strains of Beethoven's Ninth, Jane asked. 'Don't you miss your mother? You were so close to her, weren't you?'

'Not really. I mean not really to both. She brought me up to be strong and independent, not to be a leaner or a taker or a needer. She was a marvellous mother, but she wasn't very demonstrative.'

They listened to the music for a while without speaking.

Marjorie said, 'There's a woman I've had a lot to do with. She was in and out of the crisis centre. Three small children. Twenty years old. Left her husband. Something she said to me, I've never been able to forget. The possibility of us having a baby around . . . well, I just want to tell you this.'

She lay back in her chair and Jane waited.

'She's a really good mother, keeps those kids spotlessly clean, into giving them good meals, I mean *good* food, not junk stuff. She was always scared that someone from welfare would take them away from her and I said to her one day, because she didn't seem to understand what a great mother she was being, "Look, no one's going to take your children away from you, because you give them so much. You're a responsible, terrific Mum to them." '

Marjorie got up and said, 'I'll put the kettle on. Want some coffee?'

She came back and leaned against the mantelpiece over the fireplace,

'Well, she said to me, "That's not the part I'm worrying about. It's when they want to hug me, climb on my lap, kiss me, all that. I want to hug them back, I want to kiss them and say "I love you so much and I *can't*." '

Marjorie paused again, went on, 'Then she kind of shouted out at me, as though she was angry, "how can I give my children love I never had myself?" '

Jane shivered, rubbed her upper arms vigorously, said, 'Ow, that brought me out in goose pimples.'

Marjorie nodded. 'I know.'

Jane looked at her uncertainly.

'Marjorie? Are you telling me something?'

'I guess so. If you're going to have this baby, if *we're* going to have this baby, we're going to have to give it everything we've got. I don't ever want to find myself, or you, suffering the way she was suffering. She didn't have any input of love in her life and she was stuck in a really bad space. What I'm trying to say is, bringing up a child together is going to alter a lot in our lives. We're not going to be self-oriented any more . . .'

'The baby will have to be the centre . . . yes, I know that.'

'What's best for her. Or him,' she added, with a grin.

Jane said, 'Since I met Ben again, I've been thinking a lot about Bim and Rocky. Remember I told you about them? They're Mum's friend Fleur's sons.'

Marjorie nodded, and Jane went on, 'I keep wondering about them.

Well, it was as though, instead of just bungling their way through adolescence like you did and I did and somehow surviving it and coming out the other side fairly able to cope with life, they fell into this kind of big black hole, while you and I, people like us, somehow we edged around it. I keep thinking I should have been able to hang on to those boys. I should have been able to do something and yet I know there was nothing I could have done.'

Marjorie reached out and touched Jane's hand gently.

'I know, sweetie. I know the feeling. It's why I have to move away from the crisis centre. I'm burned out. I can't hack it any longer, that feeling that I should be able to help someone, even when my head is telling me no one can help anyone, when it gets down to the nitty-gritty.'

When Jane saw Ally a few days later, she was astonished at the change in her mother's appearance. Ally had been digging in the garden, threw down the spade and walked quickly to meet Jane. Everything about her was subtly different, the brightness of her eyes, the glowing smile, even a lightness in her step.

Ally was similarly surprised by what seemed to be a change in her daughter, who no longer had the faintly sulky look she'd grown to expect, but a new brightness, a glow of well-being. They looked at each other shyly, after they'd hugged, Jane wondering if it was Rowley going away that had changed her mother, or had working at the refuge so quickly raised Ally's awareness, given her a sense of worth, as it so often did to women who became involved?

Both women had a feeling of shock that wasn't at all unpleasant, in fact made them acutely curious about each other. It was like entering new territory where all the old paths had ended and the possibility existed of exciting new directions.

At first they sought common ground, sitting over a pot of tea discussing Rowley.

'I felt really angry when he went away, Mum,' Jane said. 'Not just for you but because I felt abandoned, too. I hated Verna for doing that to us and now I feel rather guilty. I'd never have wanted her dead. Poor Dad. He must feel awful. Is he coming back here, to you? I mean, do you want him back?'

'I don't know. What do you think? Do you think I ought to?' Ally's voice was suddenly nervous.

'God, Mum, don't ask me! Don't ask anyone. If he comes back it's got to be because you want him to. Not because he wants to or because you think I want him to. Do what you want.'

Ally nodded. 'Yes, I guess I've learnt that.'

Ally went on: 'I've been thinking about the old days when we lived at Gardenvale. Fancy you going back to live there.'

'I love Gardenvale. I was happy there.'

'Funny. I was lonely. I should have been lonelier when we moved here, you and Rowley were away so much. It's the ocean, the noise it makes. Like having somebody pottering around all the time.'

'Pottering around! That continual roar used to drive me nuts!'

Before lunch they walked down to the beach. Ally started telling Jane about the workshops she'd done.

'I wish we could have done some of them together, Jane.'

'Well, of course, I did all that kind of stuff when I was doing my training.'

'I know, but things that came up, would make me think, oh I wish Janey was here. We had a session about women's experiences when they begin to menstruate and it was amazing that girls of eighteen were talking about the same kind of experience I had when I started, decades ago. As though nothing was changing.' She looked shyly at her daughter. 'And I was really pleased that I'd done such a good job preparing you for it. I thought, well that's one thing I did right for Janey.'

Jane stared at her mother. 'Mum! That was one of the worst days of my life!'

'But . . . I'd talked to you about it. I'd talked to you ages before you started. What do you mean?'

'That's what I *mean*. By the time it happened, I was actually looking forward to it. You'd turned it into something I'd enjoy and it wasn't like that at all. You know, all women know, it's a bloody rotten nuisance and it always will be. I got stomach cramps and I wasn't prepared for the discomfort of wearing a pad that chafed me and the alternative, shoving something hard inside myself and always being scared it'd fall out or get lost inside where I couldn't get at it. I *hated* it, the whole business, and I thought there was something wrong with me because you'd given it such a joy-of-womanhood build-up.' Suddenly Jane stopped talking, aware of the expression on her mother's face, said contritely, 'Oh, Mum, I'm sorry. I . . .'

Ally said sharply, 'Well Jane, I'm sorry it turned out that way. It's just a pity you hadn't talked to me like that at the time.'

'Talk to you! God, Mum, when did we ever talk? I'm amazed that we're having this conversation now, actually.'

'All right. I'm not going to start making excuses for my shortcomings as a mother. I acknowledge that I had plenty, but I did the best I could at the time.'

Jane watched her mother and listened, amazed. Where had she gone, that apologetic, incoherent woman she'd known all her life, the one who got to her feet and physically removed herself from discussions and arguments. Who was this new mother, standing her ground? Jane felt a stirring of pride and delight in her.

Ally was saying, 'I suppose the reason that I misled you the way I did, was because I was so anxious it wouldn't be a shock to you, the way it was to me, the first time I menstruated.'

Jane asked, 'Why, what happened?'

'Well, I can laugh about it now, but it wasn't funny at the time. I began bleeding at school and I was scared out of my wits. I could feel something sort of squashy and wet, between my legs, then after a while something trickled down the inside of my left thigh.' She stopped for a moment, lost in memory. 'There was a girl in my class, poor kid, she had some bladder trouble and every now and then she used to wet herself . . . I thought it was happening to me.'

'What did you do?'

'Sat with my legs pressed together. My teacher was a man, to make it worse. Finally, I had to do something, so I put my hand up to be excused and sort of sidled out of the room. I was scared to look back to see if my seat was wet. Anyway, I sneaked off home, waddling along like a duck and I looked down and nearly fainted when I saw it was blood on my leg. It'd stained one of my socks.'

Jane, half laughing, half crying, hugged her mother.

'Oh, poor you, Mum. I'm sorry I sounded off like that. What happened when you got home?'

'Mum was really upset. Got me into a warm bath and tried to explain what it was all about. Actually, she wasn't too clear about it. The reason she hadn't told me before, was that she hadn't started until she was fifteen and I was only twelve, so she'd thought she had plenty of time.'

'Oh, Mum, did you ever think about the way we affect each other, generations of mothers and daughters?'

Ally said nervously, 'How did I affect you, Jane?'

Jane said, 'Do you mind if we talk about it?'

Ally shook her head. 'Why not? We've never talked like this before. Why don't we clear the air? I'm sure there're a lot of other things I bungled when I was trying to bring you up.'

'Oh, Mum. You said it before. You tried your best. God knows what a mess I'll make of being a mother . . .'

Ally looked at her sharply. Jane thought, no, not yet, it's not time yet.

She stood, stretched and yawned.

'What does a daughter have to do to get fed around here?'

As they turned towards the house and began strolling back, Ally impulsively linked her arm through Jane's. In moments, she wished she hadn't. The discomfort created by the contact was palpable. To break it, she stooped and picked up a stone, pretended to examine it.

A nervousness grew between them as they washed the dishes. They were laughing too much and Jane dropped a cup. They both stooped to pick up the pieces, Jane apologising profusely, bumped heads and laughed again.

Ally had an uncanny suspicion that Jane was pregnant, but didn't have the courage to ask her. She wondered if Ben ... it *must* have been Ben ... wondered what was going to happen if she was right. Her heart beat faster at the thought of Ben and Jane and a baby, trying to reconcile her instinct with the knowledge that, nevertheless, Jane was still living with Marjorie. Jane was wondering how to begin talking to Ally about Marjorie. Their mutual prattling was beginning to get on her nerves. She looked around and said, 'The house looks lovely, Mum. Not cluttered like it used to be. Where did all Dad's things go?'

'Oh,' Ally looked around guiltily, 'packed away.' To change the subject, she went on quickly, 'You know Mum used to tell me that her grandmother said if you make sure the corners of a room are always clean, the whole room will look tidy.'

Jane burst out laughing again.

'Really, Mum? That's a little gem you never passed on to me. Anyway, you had an awful hang-up about tidiness. The corners never had a chance to look messy with you around. You were so house proud that it turned me into a slob. I didn't want to get like you. Remember how you were always blasting me about my untidiness?'

'It wasn't me I was thinking of. It was Rowley. He was so fussy about the house.'

'But you were the one who was always dusting and polishing. It used to drive me mad the way you walked around cleaning up after people, as though someone was handing out marks for tidiness. Why did you have to be like that?'

'I don't know. I thought I had to keep everything spotless. It was all I could think of to do.'

In the silence that followed, they looked at each other. Jane looked so troubled and so beautiful to Ally that suddenly it seemed ridiculous to imagine there was a barrier between them. Gently, she reached out and touched Jane's hand.

'I've got this funny feeling that you're pregnant.'

Jane looked sixteen years old again and flushed as she'd done when Ally questioned her about some imagined wrong-doing. She nodded her head.

'Yes, I think so. Actually, you've just confirmed it, haven't you? I must be, if you noticed.'

'Darling, I'm thrilled! Can I ask . . . was it Ben?'

'It couldn't have been anyone else, Mum.'

'I'm so very glad, Janey. I was so impressed with him. A thoroughly nice young man.'

'Mum, how on earth did you know?'

'I've always been able to tell. Something about the way you look. I don't know. A kind of blooming.' She shrugged her shoulders. 'I just knew. Does he know about it – Ben?'

Jane shook her head.

'I'm not going to tell him. I meant to explain something to you and then I was going to tell you about the baby. You jumped the gun, Mum. Oh well, it doesn't matter.' She looked at her mother. 'I don't know how to say this, Mum . . .'

'Perhaps you don't have to, Jane.' The look of excitement and happiness had gone from Ally's face. The timbre of her voice had changed. There was strain in it now. 'It's Marjorie, isn't it? I wondered why you'd decided to rent a house and then you were talking about the possibility of buying it. You don't have to explain if you don't want to.'

Jane got to her feet and stood facing Ally.

'Are you running away from me, Mum? I realise how hard it must be for you. But we do have to talk about it. It's your grandchild I'm having, Mum.'

When Jane got home that night, she walked into the living-room. Marjorie was sitting on the carpet, a glass of sherry in her hand, a fire burning in the grate. Jane burst into tears.

Marjorie stood up and put her arms around her.

'Hullo, been to see your mother, have you? Didn't go so well, is that it? Nobody ever said it was going to be easy, Janey. Sit down and I'll get you a drink, and it'd better be milk, in case this baby is real.'

When Jane had stopped crying, she said, 'Oh Marjorie, if you'd seen her face when she knew about the baby. She knew before I *told* her.'

'Darling, you haven't had a pregnancy test yet. Don't you think you ought to wait for that?'

'I'm pregnant. I know. Mum knows. It's not that. It's how she looked. She was so thrilled and she guessed it was Ben and she thought everything had turned out beautifully in the end and then I had to hit her with it not being like that at all, but of course, she'd already guessed that, too, she was just clutching at the idea of Ben, the baby, me, desperately hoping the real thing would just go away.'

'Were you able to help her feel differently?'

Jane shook her head. 'No. Oh, she pretended, but I could see she was devastated. We talked for a while, it was all very sensible and civilised. Maybe it'd have been better if she'd hit me or screamed or broken dishes over my head.'

'Not really. Look, calm down. Think of the baby. It'll be all right. She'll get used to the idea. You can talk again. We can all talk again.'

'I hope she doesn't take off for America, like your Mum. I don't want her to piss off like Dad.' Jane burst into a wail. 'Oh, hell, I have to tell *him*, too.'

Seven

No use sitting there, trying to tell herself that being lesbian was another part of human rights, the same as choosing to get married or stay single, go to work or work at home having children, decide how many to have or have none at all; no use, when she was so sunk in sorrow, guilt and shock. Why shock? She'd known what was happening, the knowledge filtering in gradually, accepted reluctantly, during the years that Jane and Marjorie were becoming Jane-and-Marjorie.

When had Jane become . . . how hard it was even to think the wretched word. When had her daughter made the decision to live with and love another woman, or had it happened more accidentally, through proximity, habit, happened as slowly as her own fearful recognition of the situation?

What had gone wrong? More precisely, where had she and Rowley gone wrong? Was it because they'd never pushed religion at her, having none themselves? Was it because never until now had she and Jane been able to talk, to turn to each other for advice, confirmation, support? Perhaps if she and Rowley had loved each other more, they could have shown Jane a good marriage.

When she'd looked at Jane that day and suspected that she was pregnant, her thoughts had flown immediately to Ben. The relief had been exquisite, overwhelming, until the quiver of uncertainty, thinking of the house Jane and Marjorie had so recently rented, the talk of buying it. Jane had looked so stern later, just before she'd left, trying so hard to explain her feelings for Marjorie, and Ally had been unable to hold back the tears; it had been like a double exposure, seeing the real Jane before her, denying Ben, and in her stupid head another Jane who might have been glowing and joyous, full of excitement, the two of them planning a wedding.

What about the baby, this child coming into her life when she'd almost stopped thinking about the possibility of grandchildren? How would it feel to be so different, being brought up by two women? Not to know who your father was, though that happened to plenty of children. Jane, she thought with a flash of spite, might have a surprise coming to her in ten or fifteen years. Children could get very hung-up on tracking down a natural parent. And no matter what Jane wanted, she, Ally, knew who her grandchild's father was.

Did Jane and Marjorie mean this to be a permanent arrangement? What happened when the baby was ready for school? Did they pretend to be just two women living in the same house or did they both go along to school functions, not caring that people knew their relationship? Had they even thought that far ahead? Ally felt a surge of violence, a feeling that she wanted to assault Marjorie physically, to make her get out of Jane's life.

The first thing that Rowley would think of would be psychiatric help for Jane. Ally moaned aloud. Rowley! She'd have to ring Jane and insist that she must be the one to tell him about the baby and everything. He had to know.

At the thought of Rowley, Ally's rage changed direction. Why wasn't he here when she needed him?

Why was she blaming Rowley? Ally sat very still, breathing deeply, trying to steady down. OK she'd had her anger out, now it was time to think. Calmly and clearly. Compassionately?

Compassion. Try that. What had happened here? Jane loved

Marjorie. Marjorie must love Jane. Otherwise they wouldn't have stayed together for so long.

Love. This was about love, wasn't it? How could love be a disaster? How come she was getting into a frenzy and a panic over *love*? Jane was having a baby. Everyone involved would love the baby.

This was about *love*. Not death, not violence, fear, anger, jealousy, hate – none of those negative things.

Was love the place she could start from? She could think of no other starting point.

Something Sylvia had said one day at the refuge came back to her. Ally had been feeling drained to the point of exhaustion. Sylvia had said, 'Learn to step back, Ally. No matter how much you care, it's not your problem. You can support women more effectively when you act with your head as well as your heart.'

It wasn't her problem was it? Nor was it her right to attach blame to Marjorie. It must have been a decision they'd made together, surely? Building Marjorie up into some kind of ogre was childish.

So, if she thought compassionately about this loving situation, stepped back a little from it, didn't judge or blame those involved . . . Ally was scared she'd lose that thought. She found a notepad and wrote it down.

When she woke in the morning she lay for a moment feeling peaceful, then remembrance of Jane's visit of yesterday flooded back. She felt wretched and depressed. Sad. How different if . . . Ally threw back the bedclothes and jumped out of bed. It was pointless to think how she had been looking forward to Jane and Ben getting married, absolutely, finally, stupidly pointless. Where the hell had she put that bit of paper? She found it on the kitchen table and sat down and read it, muttering, be compassionate, be loving, step back, don't blame, don't be judgemental. Ask Jane and Marjorie to dinner? Not today. No, but next week. Today she was going to go and see Fleur, break the rules, those unspoken rules that had insinuated themselves over the years.

Hoping that the wretched Swain would be gone, Ally pressed the button and heard the musical chimes ring inside. When Fleur opened the door, Ally was surprised to see she was heavily made-up, even though it was early in the day. She kissed her friend and said anxiously, 'Hope it's OK, calling in like this?'

'Of course it is.' Fleur peered at Ally, 'What's wrong?'

'Nothing! Are you all right?'

Fleur turned away quickly.

'Of course I am. Had a migraine last night, that's all. My eyes still feel puffy.'

Ally would have accepted that, for Fleur did have migraines now and then, usually after drinking too much red wine, but, as she turned away, the loose sleeve of her dress fell back from her upper arm, revealing an ugly bruise. Ally drew in her breath sharply.

'Who did that?'

'What? Oh, for heaven's sake, Swain and I were fooling around! Are you going to turn into a pain in the bum now you're working at a refuge, Ally? Like some coffee?'

'Please.'

Over coffee, Ally told Fleur the news of Verna's death in the car accident, of Rowley's homecoming.

'I can't say I liked Verna, but I wouldn't have wished her dead. What a shock for poor old Rowley.'

Fleur was sitting facing the light from the window. Under the make-up Ally saw that one of her eyes was quite badly bruised. Leaning forward, she said, 'Fleur, what happened? It's not just your arm. Your eye is bruised.'

She saw that she'd made Fleur angry. Fleur said coldly, 'Back off, Ally. I'm not one of your refuge cases.'

'It's nothing to do with the refuge, Fleur. You're my friend. How couldn't I be concerned when I see bruises on you?'

'You want me to tell you all about it, do you? Well, that's very funny. Ha, ha, There've been times when I was dying to talk to you, Ally, really talk to you, not just natter and gossip like we always did and, Ally, every time you'd get up and run away from me. I could never get started. You didn't want to know and now, just because you do something at a bloody women's refuge, you want to pry into my life. Well, how about you talk to me about your life, Ally, your problems? How come you didn't tell me Ben visited you? I had a card from him the other day and that was the first I knew he'd been here and people we both know keep telling me you were as nutty as a fruit cake after Rowley left and you got as fat as a pig, so you talk to me about your life, Ally, huh?'

Ally's face was burning, her heart thudding. Fleur had never spoken to her like that before.

'I'm sorry. I didn't mean . . . all right, I did want to, oh, sort of, be helpful. You're right, I was being nosey. I won't do it again. Sorry! And I don't know why I forgot to tell you about Ben, I honestly meant to. He's turned into a nice young man, not a bit plump like he used to be.'

Ally had an intense and desperate desire to pour it all out to Fleur, all her anxieties and doubts, but before she could begin, Fleur had interrupted. When had they both become so expert at doing that?

'Actually, Ally, I'm glad I was away. Oh, I'd like to have seen him again, he was a cute little kid, but he'd have wanted to know about Bim and Rocky and I wouldn't have known what to say. Did he ask about them?'

Ally nodded. 'I just said they were travelling around somewhere up north.'

'He was quite keen on Jane when they were all kids.'

'Yes. He asked after her.'

'I suppose he's married anyway?' Ally nodded and changed the subject. The impulse to confide in Fleur had passed.

'I don't know how I feel about Rowley coming home.'

'Does he expect to come back to you?'

'I don't know.'

'Do you want him back?'

'I don't know that either. I'm feeling confused, Fleur.'

'Oh, well, I suppose you'll know when you see him. Listen, Ally, I don't want you to get the wrong idea about Swain. I'm sorry I sounded off like that before. All that happened was we had a bit too much to drink and I kept provoking him and finally he just socked me a couple of times. Served me right. I asked for it.'

Ally said awkwardly, 'Oh. Oh, that's how it was.'

Fleur burst out laughing. 'God, Ally, you're such a little prude. You always have been. How on earth do you handle it at the refuge?'

Ally laughed. 'Well, it's a shock to the system, but, I dunno, I seem to manage OK. I make some of the women laugh, so that's good. Anything for a laugh at a place like that.'

'Anyway, Swain's gone for good. I told him not to come back. I was sick of him. I mean, he was fantastically hung and all that, but pretty rough in the sack. Real wham-bang operator. I got fed up. Who needs that type?'

Ally felt nervous. Why was Fleur being so crude? It wasn't like her.

'I know what you're thinking. When you met him you were worried and you thought Fleur's such a sucker for common chaps like this. Well, I get lonely, Ally. You'll find out what it's like, unless you take Rowley back. It can get very lonely without a man around. If you don't want Rowley, I might snaffle him myself.' She grinned. 'At least I'd be sure he wasn't going to sock me in the eye.'

Ally smiled, 'No, Rowley's gentle, I'll say that for him. I must say, I appreciate him a lot more, now I'm at the refuge and finding out what some women have to put up with.'

After she'd left, Ally still felt shocked by her visit to Fleur. She had a strange feeling that this wasn't the first time Fleur had been hit by a man. For a while, Fleur had looked and sounded like a stranger and Ally had seemed to get a fleeting glimpse of a part of her friend's life she'd never dreamed of. She felt disturbed. Then she slowed to a stop to let a young woman with a pram cross the road, and began thinking of Jane again.

Ally was working three days a week at the refuge. Sometimes during a crisis she was called in on her off days, or she'd go in just to have a cup of coffee and stay a while. The refuge had quickly become the centre of her life. It was hard to realise how isolated she'd felt before. Why had she never investigated community facilities? She hadn't known such places existed. Not only was there the refuge, but resource centres as well; all kinds of activities where a woman such as she'd been could find company and things to do. No one was without value.

How nearly she'd missed discovering all the things she was now finding out she could do – real skills that had gone unnoticed all her life.

Two nights after she'd visited Fleur, there was a knock at the door. Ally jumped. The ocean was pounding in on a full tide and a high wind was blowing. She hadn't heard a car drive in. Fleur was at the door, with a swollen jaw.

'Now listen,' she said sharply, when Ally gasped. 'Shut the damned door, for goodness sake, that wind's cold. Listen, Ally, don't make a fuss, OK? I've been to the hospital and my jaw's not broken. It's only swollen.' She smiled, with difficulty. 'I told them I was mugged. Do you get mugged in Parktown or is that only New York?'

Before Ally could answer, Fleur went on, 'Just don't make a fuss. I've been like this before; all I want is company and a cup of tea.'

'Right, that's what you'll have.'

Ally put the jug on.

'Am I allowed to ask if it was Swain?'

'Yes. It was Swain. He's gone again. Actually, I think I broke his nose.'

Ally stared at her slender, petite friend.

'*How*?'

Fleur's eyes danced.

'Remember those heavy Swedish rolling-pins we bought that time and I said they'd make good weapons if you were ever attacked?' Ally nodded. 'Well, I was attacked, wasn't I, and I just happened to lay my hands on the rolling-pin, so I let him have it, zonko on the conko.'

'Why don't you come and work at the refuge, we could do with someone like you there?'

'No way! Definitely not my scene. Besides, it would discourage the customers, to see one of the helpers coming in looking like this.'

She took the cup Ally handed to her.

'It's funny, Ally. I feel a lot closer to you than I used to. I often wanted to come running to you, but I was scared of what you'd think of me.' She grinned. 'Ouch! that hurts. You know that old joke . . . only when I laugh?'

Ally nodded.

Fleur said, 'What I mean is, I don't need a thing from you, Ally, but it's really nice to be able to come and see you, even when I look like the walking wounded. Before, I wouldn't have dreamed of letting you see me like this. I felt silly, to say the least.'

Ally nodded. 'You got through that tea fast. Like another cup?'

Fleur nodded and Ally got up again. Once it would have unnerved her to have Fleur sitting there with her swollen jaw, her eye still bruised. Ally's heart would have been pounding, her throat feeling thick, her words, if they came at all, coming out all wrong, terrified because she didn't know what was expected of her. Now, she realised with surprise, she was feeling relaxed, because she'd been freed of the need to do anything about Fleur, except to be there for whatever Fleur wanted of her. It was so comfortable.

Fleur stayed the night with Ally.

'I suppose it'd be sensible,' she admitted when Ally suggested it. 'Swain just might come back again. I'll get the lock changed again tomorrow. I'm always getting locks changed. Nutty, isn't it?'

Ally had the feeling that she and Fleur were like two canoeists who'd just negotiated a tricky set of rapids and were now settling down in a good, strong, smooth flow, paddling on in unison. How superficial their relationship had been before; while thinking of themselves as close friends, best friends, they had been too afraid to confide in each other.

Rowley coming back . . . how was that going to affect things? Ally rolled restlessly on to her other side. She couldn't afford Rowley. It boiled down to that. How could she possibly proceed with this amazing life, this daring, new, exciting life, if he expected a return to their old pattern? He'd made his choice, she'd made hers. That was something he couldn't have counted on, that she'd finish up making a choice, too. His had gone disastrously wrong. Hers was progressing just fine.

A few days later she was at the airport, watching him walk towards her, that tall, slender man with the worn, handsome face, shoulders just a little stooped.

Rowley put his suitcase down and hugged her to him. Ally went very still. In the car, she turned to him, said abruptly, 'Where would you like to be dropped, Rowley?'

He stared at her, shock in his eyes.

'Rowley?'

'I thought I'd be going out to the beach house with you.'

More gently, she answered, 'It doesn't suit me to have you there, Rowley. I'm working now and I feel I'd rather live alone.'

Rowley looked hurt, said quietly, 'I need you.'

It upset her. Humility wasn't his style.

'Rowley . . .'

'Ally. Please. I need to come home. I couldn't face a hotel room tonight. I've been under a terrible strain. I don't know who else I could go to.'

Was compassion to be confined to the women she supported at the refuge? She never looked at the rights and wrongs of what had happened to them; they came for support and she gave it to them, unquestioningly. Wasn't Rowley suffering as they did, weren't his eyes pleading for understanding, as theirs did? Suddenly she remembered the man she'd watched on the beach that day . . . Everyman. Rowley was Everyman, too. Ally sighed.

'All right, Rowley. Of course you can come home.'

They spoke little that night. She meant to put him into the spare room, but he walked into the main bedroom as though he'd been away on a normal business trip. When she'd finished washing the cups, after they'd had hot cocoa, he was in bed, already asleep.

Ally made up the spare bed and, disgruntled, slept there, restlessly. When she woke the room was full of cool, grey, dawn light. She slipped from bed, put on a track suit and went for her walk.

How sad that, at the cost of Verna's life, Ally had now discovered she didn't need Rowley in her life. It seemed to have happened overnight. She'd gone to sleep, feeling confused and unhappy, and woken sure of herself and her needs and her right to choose whether Rowley returned or was sent away. And right now, she thought, stamping up the back steps, not bothering to brush the sand from her feet before entering the house, now she was bloody annoyed to have Rowley there when all she wanted to do was eat her breakfast while reading a book and keeping an ear open to the morning radio news. Rowley was, as she'd feared, sitting at the kitchen table.

Briskly, she said, 'Hi. I have to go out for the day soon, Rowley.'

'Oh yes, you're working, you said. I'm glad you were able to find something. What are you doing?'

Ally took a deep breath: 'There's no money involved yet, but I'll be going on the paid staff as soon as funding improves. It's at a refuge. A women's refuge, just over in Parktown.'

Rowley stared, then laughed.

'You're kidding! A women's refuge in *Parktown*?'

'Why would I kid you about that? Believe me, Rowley, Parktown these days has got all the problems of any other place that's grown fast. It's worse, in a way, because the community was so unprepared to handle such a volume of domestic problems as there is now.'

'Well, Ally, that puts a different complexion on your job. I don't like the thought of you working at a place like that . . .'

'Like what? What do you know about refuges?' she said sharply.

Rowley had a hard look in his eyes.

'A place that's run by aggressive women, tough women, lesbians, activists. I knew you'd changed, Ally, as soon as I saw you at the airport.'

Ally had forgotten her own initial fears of the place.

'You're talking off the top of your head, Rowley. You wouldn't have a clue. You have to work there to know what it's like. I work with really terrific women and I don't give a damn what you or anyone likes to think. If you feel threatened by the concept of refuges for women, then that's your problem.'

Ally went to work that day, still shaking with rage. She and Rowley had argued loudly and, of course, inevitably they had begun to rake up anger from the past, anger that had always been repressed, unacknowledged. Finally, she'd gone to her room, slamming the door behind her, dressed quickly and gone breakfastless to work, her parting shot telling Rowley she expected him to be gone when she returned late that afternoon and that they had nothing further to discuss. He'd shouted after her, 'We've got plenty to discuss, Ally. I don't want my name to be connected with what you're doing in Parktown!' and she'd screamed at the top of her voice, 'Shut up!' and driven off with gravel flying from under the wheels of her car. Two miles down the road she wondered how Rowley was going to leave when she'd gone off and stranded him without transport. The hell with it, she thought, let him ring for a taxi. She'd let Rowley return home out of pity, and had meant to be kind and gentle with him. Well, he hadn't changed and she had. That was it. End of story. There was no going back for either of them. Let him find someone else and this time he'd be a bit more careful who he chose, someone who'd be glad to look up to him and respect his judgement. Damned if she was willing to be like that any more.

It was almost nine in the evening when Ally drove home, relieved to see that the house was dark. Rowley had gone, then. An hour later she remembered she hadn't looked in the mailbox. Taking her torch she walked down to the gate. The box was empty. She need not have bothered, she didn't get much mail. Back at the house she started to close the door before turning off the outside light, when she noticed something glint briefly under the spreading branches of a large tree.

Strange, what could be catching the light over in that corner of the garden? The moon hadn't risen. Stars shone briefly as scattered clouds drifted. Something had glinted and she couldn't think what it was. A leaf, perhaps, damp from dew, on a twig drooping lower than the others? A damp leaf catching the starlight?

Ally shrugged and closed the door. She made sure the chain was in place and went around the house checking locks. Everything was calm and still, the ocean sighing and grating on the pebbles washed up as the tide came in.

She had a long shower and went to bed. At ten past three in the morning she woke; she'd been dreaming of Rowley and she woke with a feeling of grief. Ally switched on the reading lamp and groped for her book. She wasn't going to lie getting herself into a stew over things. What had happened had happened. Let it be. Sleep didn't come. She kept reading the same line over and over again. She went to the kitchen and heated a glass of milk, carried it through the house and stood looking down over the trees to the ocean.

The earlier clouds had cleared. In the light from the risen moon she clearly saw someone standing on the beach. Her heart gave a frightened bump and quickly she retreated into the house. Someone was down there, someone tall and bulky, motionless, faintly outlined against the moonglow reflected from the water. The figure moved and something glinted, the same kind of glint that had attracted her attention earlier.

Ally watched through the window. As though her gaze had been communicated, the figure began to move slowly away towards the headland.

She sensed now that it was a man. The glint came again, briefly. What could it be? A gun? No, guns were dark-barrelled, weren't they? A knife? Someone with a metal hand, she thought wildly. Oh the hell with it. Wearily, she went back to bed. On the edge of sleep, it came to her. The head of an axe, hung low, swinging in the hand, would glint like that. An axe, held low, swung loose, with shining, honed-bright edge. Terrified, she sat up. The axeman, the one who'd rung the refuge and that she'd read about in the daybook weeks ago!

He could have followed her home. But no one could have followed her along the last stretch of dirt road without her seeing him. Suppose he'd followed once, seen where she turned off the highway, then, next time, was waiting there, car parked near the turn-off, out of sight. She drove the dirt section slowly. He could have kept up with her, running silently through the trees. There were only two houses set well back on one side of the road, then hers.

Why her? Why the Parktown refuge? Had there some time been a woman sheltering there whose husband was an axeman? Some man whose woman had left him, maybe had him sent to gaol, spurned him, divorced him, got custody of the kids, learned to stand on her own feet?

Already she was familiar with the terrible rage of the outsmarted male who was well aware that alone his woman wouldn't have known how to protect herself legally against his violence. A raging bull, knowing he'd been outwitted by not just one cow, but a bunch of them.

If he'd been selecting one of the refuge workers, cutting her out from the herd, she'd be the one, living alone in this isolated place.

Was she being paranoid? She'd thought, at first, all refuge workers tended that way. But she'd found out the violence was there, it existed, directed as much at them, the protectors and supporters, as against the women who went to the house for refuge. She'd heard the fury in those voices... the phone call that very first day... felt the hatred aimed at her, was shocked to know she was the object of a man's wild anger, she, gentle Ally who'd never hurt anyone in her life, who wasn't trying to get back at men, for no man had ever raised a hand to her in anger.

But an *axe*, a hand swinging an axe? It couldn't be. Yet she lay sleepless until blessed dawn filled the room with its lovely light. She went from window to window, looking out on to a peaceful world, uninhabited as far as she could see. She made a cup of tea, drank it sitting up in bed. Reassured, she fell asleep.

Later that day, at the refuge, she took a phone call from an inner city refuge. Could Parktown take in a pregnant woman? The caller, whose name was Billie, said she'd bring the woman down straight away.

Ally had wanted to tell Heather about the drama of her night, but there had been no time. In the surge of emergency events the day was bringing, it had receded to the back of her mind.

No more than eighteen, Justina had tousled, red hair, curling lavishly down her back, a small, freckled face, anxious blue-green eyes. She wore a cotton dress with a heavy sweater over it and her feet were in sandals, in spite of the chill of the day. After Billie had left, Ally rummaged in a box of winter clothes that had been brought in that day, found some that looked like Justina's size, as well as a pair of well-worn, sheepskin-lined boots.

The girl's pregnancy was well advanced. Between gasps and pauses while Justina blew her running nose, she told Ally she'd been going with one special man since schooldays. At sixteen, he'd started shooting up heroin. She'd thought she could get him off it. As time slipped by, he got worse, until she could scarcely recognise him as the boy she'd loved for so long.

'I still love him,' she said mournfully, 'but it's no use. It's not even his baby, you know?'

Hugh, her man, had needed a fix desperately one day. Neither of them had any money. Ally hadn't asked where they usually got it from. By then she understood the story only too well. There were ways to get money, all of them terrible.

'Have you ever seen someone needing a fix, Ally?' Ally nodded. She knew that now, too. They'd had a heroin addict in only the week before.

'It's awful, isn't it, the way they shake and scratch themselves and jerk around. I couldn't stand it. There was this creepy guy, one of the pushers, I knew he fancied me, so when he called in, I said he could fuck me if he fixed Hugh up first. Well, I didn't think I'd get pregnant from just once, you know? I was desperate to help Hugh. I couldn't bear to watch him the way he was. Then, when I found out about the baby, it sort of cleared my head out. It was a really good thing because it meant I had someone else to worry about, a little kid that had never hurt anyone, kind of relying on me to do the right thing by him. I just feel so tender about this baby . . . I looked at Hugh and I felt real sad, but I could help the baby and I couldn't help Hugh, so it made it easy to go. I'm all this baby's got going for it. If Hugh ever kicks the habit, he'll find me, I know he will. He understands why I had to go. The only thing is, knowing a lot about pushers and all that, I got into the refuge to be safe.'

That was why Billie had brought her over from the other refuge and why they'd have to move her out to a safe place. Sometimes, people searching for a woman would get another to pose as a crisis case to get someone inside so they could check who was there. When Lynsey came in, she said friends of hers had a place up in the hills that they wanted to let. It sounded ideal. She phoned Gillie, one of her friends, at the hospital where she worked.

Sylvia approved of the idea and Ally was to drive the girl up in the refuge car as quickly as possible. The drive took her to a part of the peninsula she knew well. Justina seemed nervous, so Ally talked to her about the old couple she'd visited as a child. High on a bare mountain, they lived in an old farmhouse with a million-dollar view.

'They had a horse called, oh, what was his name? Something very manly and solid, what was it? Bert? Alfred? Dick? Ha, Dicken, that was it.'

She smiled, telling Justina how the buggy wheels made a noise, a crunchy, sugary noise she could still remember so clearly.

'They were friends of Mum's grandmother, I think. We used to go and visit them about once a year when I was about seven. We'd go in the buggy down to the beach.'

Ally and Beth, running down the coarse sand of the beach, plunging into the sea, screaming at the coldness, leaping about and peering down to see if any lurking crabs were about to nip their toes. And the exquisite agony of trying to rub the sand from their feet before they left. She'd never understood then, but it must have been granite sand, the texture was so rough and hard. She remembered the icy numbness of her feet, the struggle it had been to get socks and shoes on again, fingers numb from long immersion in that chilly sea.

Justina was glancing at her curiously. She smiled at the girl.

'I was just thinking about it, the fun I used to have with my sister.'

No pain. There'd been no pain in the remembrance of Beth that time. Justina was saying, 'You're lucky. I never had a sister.'

Strange how women who came into the refuge nearly always assumed that you'd never known suffering, had no problems of your own.

The house they reached was perched on a shelf of land overlooking Parktown. Viran, who lived there with Gillie, was at home and walked out on to the wide veranda to greet them. He was assistant matron at the district hospital and Gillie was a midwifery sister at a maternity hospital. He smiled, 'Looks as though we're just the neighbours you needed, Justina.'

It was a big, old-fashioned house, wrapped around with verandas and divided into two self-contained flats. There was no electricity and Justina brushed this aside as of no importance in her joy at sighting five acres of orchard and garden and vegetable plot. Viran and Gillie were asking only thirty dollars a week and she could manage that on her social security benefit.

The girl became ecstatic in her praise of everything she looked at; she said she couldn't wait for the baby to be born so she'd be in better shape to kneel and get her hands into the earth.

'I love gardening! It's one thing I just love. Oh, this is just meant to be, I know it is. I'll be so happy here.'

Ally said she'd come by the following day, to take Justina to the charity shop.

'They'll probably find a telly for you and a radio, might even have a kerosene fridge. We'll see what they've got.'

Back at the refuge, the scene had mercifully quietened. Lynsey and Sylvia were sprawled in the office drinking coffee. Ally got herself a mug and told them of her experience the night before.

'Do you think I'm going nuts?' she asked anxiously.

'I sure as hell don't,' said Sylvia, getting up and rummaging in the filing cabinet.

'Look, here's the two original daybooks. Have a skim through them. See if you can find any reference to a woman whose bloke had something to do with axes. Like a timber-getter or a champion axeman, you know those guys who go in for competitions? I can't recall anyone like that but you just might pick up a clue.'

'Hang on,' Lynsey went to the cabinet. 'Before you do that, look through this one. In the remarks column. Anything specially interesting was recorded there. It's the old admittance ledger. Every case involving violence has a V against it. That'll break it down a bit for you.'

Ally pored over the books for the rest of the day. No reference to an axe-wielding man, sane or crazy, except for that one threatening phone call. She put the books away, depressed and appalled by the experiences that had been written in them, smiling a little, too, at the vein of humour that ran through everything, as though the only way the writer had been able to endure it was to crack a joke whenever she could.

It was all based on so little, what she'd been searching for; a glint under a tree in a dark place, the bulk of an unknown figure on the beach. Surely, to build that into the menace of a deranged, axe-armed avenger required too big a leap from known facts, too great a leap to think of talking to the police about it, some of whom regarded the refuge staff as hopeless overreactors. As Lynsey had said, they'd overreact, too, dammit, if the physical requirement for a cop was five foot four and eight stone.

When Ally drove home, the events of the morning seemed a long way away, as though they'd happened to another woman in another place. Fleur's car was in the driveway and her friend was strolling up through the trees towards the house, a dog by her side, a young alsatian.

Fleur broke into a run and the dog gambolled along, pink tongue flapping, foolish grin on his young face.

'Here, Ally,' Fleur called, out of breath, 'come and get him. He's yours.'

Surprised, Ally took the leash from Fleur.

'For me? I'm not sure I want a dog, Fleur.'

'Listen, mate, I was scared stiff that night I stayed with you. It's too lonely out here. It's not safe, Ally. I didn't want to say anything to you until I got the dog, but I made up my mind that night, I'd see you had some protection. I got this pooch from friends of mine. He's a really good dog and if you give him a bit of training, he'll be as good as having the police force on your doorstep.'

'Heaven forbid,' Ally murmured. She'd always liked dogs. Strange she'd never got herself one. When she opened the door, she slipped the leash from around his neck and the dog crashed inside, bushy tail knocking small objects flying as he skidded on the polished wooden floor.

Ally muttered, 'Oh great, I can tell Rowley the dog broke the vase, if he ever notices it's gone.'

'What's that?' Fleur asked.

'Forget it. Not important. I'm not sure I can handle this, Fleur. Look at those paws. This dog's going to be enormous. What am I going to call you, dog?'

The pup wagged his tail enthusiastically and a book went flying from a low shelf. He had silver markings, the rest of him a blend of glossy black and silvery-grey.

'I've got it! Waldo! That's what I'll call him. Here, Waldo.'

The pup thumped his tail on the floor.

'Smart, too. Look at that. He knows his name already.'

Later, stirring her coffee, Fleur said, 'You never talk about the refuge, Ally. You really must see life there.'

'Yes, I do. I can't talk about it, Fleur, It's a confidentiality thing.'

Fleur nodded.

'Uh-huh, yes, it'd have to be like that, wouldn't it?' She gave a little sniff. 'Nothing I tell you would shock you now anyway.' She glanced at Ally, then at her cup, stirring vigorously, then put the spoon down. 'You probably think I lead a really dangerous life.'

'Well, it always has bothered me a bit, the way you let people, men, stay with you, without knowing much about them.'

'Ally, I know you think you had a rather sad childhood . . . little things you've let drop now and then . . . but did you ever wonder what kind of childhood I had? You don't know, do you? Well, compared to mine, yours would have been a fucking fairytale. Do you know, I got knocked around all the time? My Dad used to try and get into bed with me, from when I was about six . . .'

For a moment she looked quickly at Ally, then went on, 'Oh, he never succeeded, because I could run like the wind. I should have gone into athletics. I'd have been another Raelene Boyle, I bet. I never got any damned sleep, though. Always had one ear cocked for Dad's footsteps.' She gave a funny little grin, after another glance at Ally. 'The look on your face is why I've never been able to talk to you before. You just never thought I'd had that kind of childhood, did you? Well, Dad used to get so mad when he caught me, that he'd belt me up. Maybe I just got used to an exciting life, I don't know. But I can look after myself. I've been doing that since I was fifteen, when I left home for good. Don't worry about me. I'm not likely to change now, am I?'

Fleur's eyes were glittering rather strangely. Ally suddenly wondered if Fleur was schizophrenic, and dismissed the thought at once. She'd never known a saner woman. She said weakly, 'I just thought you came from pretty much the same kind of background as I did.'

'You were supposed to, kiddo. I fooled everyone. I fooled Arthur, too. He didn't have a clue about my family. He only ever met Mum, I made sure of that. I wasn't going to stick around being poor all my life, so I copied people I wanted to be like and by the time I met Arthur and made up my mind to marry him and get the kind of life I wanted for myself, you'd never have known I came from the bloody gutter.'

Ally looked at her and didn't say anything, didn't know what to say. Fleur went on with a grin, 'The only hitch was, Arthur was so dead boring. I had plenty of money and no excitement. I used to try and start fights with him, but he was like you, he used to run away and finally he ran away and stayed away.'

Fleur laughed heartily. Ally stared at her.

'Poor old Arthur. I shouldn't laugh. You know what was the last straw for him, though?' She laughed again. 'Well, you know how big

Arthur was, six foot four and built like a weight-lifter? Everything around him had to be big, except for me, his little wife, so fragile and dainty, made a nice contrast I suppose. But, you remember, he always had big cars, big swimming pool? Oh, God, I shouldn't tell you this. It's not fair to poor old Arthur. He had this *little* dick. I got such a shock the first time I saw it. Just didn't go with the rest of him. Not that it mattered. It's only men that think size is important. And did he think size was important, oh boy, he used to worry about it. Where are the tissues, Ally, I've got a sniffley nose.'

Ally reached for the box and passed it to her. Fleur blew her nose vigorously. Ally was trying desperately to relax. Why did her stomach always go so clenched when people confided in her?

Fleur went on, 'That's better. Anyway, I'd been out shopping this day, spending up big as usual, Arthur loved me spending up big,' she grinned, 'and I came home early, because I felt a bit nauseous, thought I might be pregnant again. I just made it home and I ran like mad for the bathroom, me and my Olympic sprint, and I guess Arthur didn't even hear me coming, because the door crashed open and I pelted past him to the toilet, left him frozen to the spot, stark naked, holding a tape measure, with this little erection of his, measuring the poor little thing. I was so embarrassed, I pretended I hadn't noticed, just vomited away behind him. Anyway, I guess that was the very last straw because it was only a week or so later we had a terrible fight and he just packed his things and went.'

Ally began to laugh. Fleur's story had horrified her, yet she couldn't stop laughing, almost hysterically. Every time she tried to stop, she saw a mental picture of the whole thing. Poor Arthur. She and Rowley wondered why he'd gone out of their lives so completely and finally. Rowley had been quite offended, couldn't understand why he'd severed the connection with his friends, had been half inclined to blame Ally for it, though how he could do that she'd never understood. Fleur was staring at her. Ally finally regained control of herself and Fleur said, 'Well, I thought it was funny, too, in an awful sort of way. I thought you'd be more shocked than amused, Ally.'

Ally said apologetically, 'Look, it's the whole thing, Fleur. Oh, darling, we've known each other so long and we haven't known each other at all, have we?'

She got up and went to the sink, splashed water on her face, said, as she mopped it with a towel, 'Fleur, what about your mother. Did she know what your father was trying to do to you, why you kept running from him?'

'Of course she did! They always do. Some of them, a lot of them, pretend they don't know what's going on. Don't ask me why. I never figured that one out. You'd think a woman would kill her old man when she discovered he was sleeping with her kid, or trying to, wouldn't you? Mum would just belt me when I told her, so I learned to shut up about it. No help there.'

'Yet you go to her now, when things go wrong with a man.'

'Oh, don't pussyfoot around, Ally. When I get bashed up, you mean. Yes, I go down to see Mum. It really upsets her. And that's probably why I go, isn't it? Make her pay. Don't need to be a shrink to figure that out, do you?'

'Oh Fleur. She's an old woman now.'

'Don't give me the bleeding heart bit, Ally. Besides, I had to have somewhere to go. I couldn't come to you.'

'You did this time, Fleur.'

'Yes, because you've changed, haven't you?'

Ally moved over to Fleur and put her arms around the friend who'd been her only friend for so many years. She felt tears in her eyes.

'Fleur, why didn't you tell me? Why was I the sort of person you couldn't talk to? I feel terrible about that. You needed me and I was no use to you.'

Fleur pulled away.

'Look, I don't want your pity, Ally. I've felt sorry for you for years. You led such an incredibly boring life, compared to mine.'

Ally sat back on her heels. Ouch, another hit.

'I'm not pitying you, Fleur. I don't give a damn about the way you live, or anyone lives, not now. It doesn't alter *us*, what we've been to each other, however inadequate I've been, all these years. I was the one who needed *you*. When you weren't there, I fell apart. If you hadn't come back when you did, I'd probably be in a loony bin by now, do you realise that?' Fleur shook her head. 'Well, it's true. You came back as I was about to give up. I'd had it. I couldn't handle my life any more. So it's not pity I feel for you. You're the best friend I've ever had, Fleur. We've both got through life the best way we could. We're OK. Both of us. We're bloody little miracles. Survivors, both of us. I need you, Fleur.'

Fleur said, 'Just as long as you don't expect me to change and as long as you don't nag me when I go on living how I want to.'

In bed that night (Fleur had left after they'd given each other a rare, shy kiss), Ally lay awake for a long time, trying to reconcile in her mind the Fleur she thought she'd known all those years, with the real Fleur, now unmasked. Again Ally was appalled at the extent of her failure to observe what was happening to those closest to her, frightened for Fleur who was stuck in a looping kind of life pattern that continually swung her back into dangerous situations.

She had a funny feeling. Her life had flowed so swiftly into dangerous areas. All around her people were living in a rich, crazy kind of way and she was moving through it fearfully, somehow untouched, and the thought came to her that this might change, for she was no longer an onlooker. Now she was a participator in life and sooner or later something was going to happen to her, nothing was surer than that. What it might be, how it might come, she had not the slightest idea, just this strange hunch, some sort of premonition of imminent danger.

The feeling grew so strong that she got out of bed and made herself cocoa. After that she kept waking until light grew in the east and, with it, a feeling of security.

Eight

On the Sunday of that week, Ally slept unusually late. Waldo woke her, barking and yipping frantically. From deep sleep, her eyes flew open in fright and the dog was on the bed with her, pressed as close as he could squash himself. Through eyes still blurred and unfocused, she saw a figure in the doorway and her heart leapt in terror. Then she heard Rowley's voice.

'Good god, where did you get the pup?'

'Rowley! Rowley, what the hell are you doing here?'

'Well thanks for the warm welcome. Is that supposed to be a watchdog? Better get a refund, don't you think?'

'He's only a puppy. He'll change as he gets older, don't worry. Good boy, Waldo,' she soothed him gently, 'good boy.'

Ally tipped the dog on to the floor and, still angry, went on, 'You listen to me, Rowley. Once before you caused me a lot of distress, walking into my home uninvited and unannounced. Now either you give me your keys or I'm going to have to get the locks changed. It's bloody frightening to wake up and see a man standing over me.'

'Christ, woman, I'm not *a man*, I'm still your husband. Do what you like, if that's the way you feel.'

'Oh Rowley, don't you see? Simple good manners are involved but apart from that, there's reason for me to be jumpy about intruders . . .'

'You're certainly asking for trouble, working at a refuge.'

Rowley stood stiffly in the doorway and Ally's anger evaporated, a feeling of despair replacing it.

Rowley said, 'I've been hearing a lot about your refuge and none of it's good. I'm buggered if I want my name associated with it.'

Ally was furious again. How was it that Rowley had the power to make her moods swing as they were doing, when for so long they'd been switched off from each other?

'Your damned name isn't connected with it. We only use first names, never surnames. Anyway, I can soon fix that. I'll change my bloody name . . .'

'Do you have any idea what kind of reputation that place has got, Ally? Women who go there are called sluts. I had some of them pointed out to me and I don't understand you mixing with women like that.'

'Huh, you've been drinking at the Parktown pub have you then? Yes, well, some of our residents go there to relax and we're not overjoyed about that but we don't run a reform school, you know and, OK, they're not all beautiful people but, Rowley, at least they've got the guts to try and make changes in their lives.'

'Have you got any idea how much public money is being poured into your goddamned refuges? Did you ever wonder just how much tax I have to pay every year? Oh no, of course you didn't. You've never been interested in my financial problems, have you? Never had to be, did you? The money's always been there for you. The government gets more out of every dollar I earn than I do and that's what they use to build your bloody welfare state, supporting women who can't be bothered to make a go of their marriages . . .'

'Jesus!' Ally shouted, 'I won't take any more money from you. I'll go on to a deserted wives' pension, you bastard.'

Rowley shouted as loudly, 'You will not! How dare you suggest such a thing? Do you think I haven't got any pride? All right. All right. I'm sorry I flew off the handle. I suppose what's really bothering me is I don't like you working where there's an element of danger. You could be *hurt*, Ally.'

'Rowley, I don't want to fight with you, either. I want you to understand. It isn't really like you think or like you've heard around the town. That's male prejudice, hurt pride. Men seem to think it's a slur on them, personally, that there's a need for women's refuges.' Rowley looked at her moodily. She went on: 'I think men need refuges, too. Only they don't care as much about each other as we do, not yet, anyway.'

She wanted to get up and shake him. He stood there so stiffly.

'Rowley? There's so much pain and fear and depression. Teenage girls, dying inside for want of someone to love them and care about them. Lovely girls, like Jane, clinging for years to some worthless junkie because he's all they've got.' Why wouldn't he react to what she was saying? 'Coming in to the place . . . they've never got any decent luggage, it's always old suitcases, bulging open, tied up with bits of rope. Rowley, they're so pale and sick, under-nourished. Rowley, what is wrong with you, can't you understand what I'm telling you? Don't you care, Rowley, don't you feel anything for their pain? It's real people I'm talking about. Maybe they do find it easier to hate than to love, but you've never listened and heard what their lives are like. It's the kids who get to me. Some nights I'm so tired I'm aching to go to sleep and I keep waking up and wondering what's going to happen to the children. Rowley, I saw a terrible thing happen one night. This woman was in the refuge with her kids, because her husband was violent. He'd not only beaten her, he'd beaten her son, too. He was eight years old. I had the baby in a basket in the office with me. She was three weeks old and she was crying and suddenly the little boy came running in with his arms above his head and his fists clenched and, Rowley, if I hadn't been there, he'd have beaten that tiny baby, do you see the pattern? It was what he . . .'

Rowley had turned and walked out of the room. Ally stared after him, then slid down in the bed. He didn't come back. After a while she got out and pulled on a dressing-gown. He was sitting at the kitchen table, drinking a cup of tea. Waldo was under the table, his head on Rowley's foot.

'Don't you forget you have to register the dog with the council, Ally. He's quite a nice-looking pup. What's his name?'

Ally stared at him in amazement. That was it, then. Absolutely no reaction to what she'd been saying, talking away in there, pouring it all out to him.

'I called him Waldo.'

'That was a movie. *The Great Waldo Pepper*.'

'Oh, so it was! That's where I got it from.'

'I'll take him for a walk, if you like.'

Rowley tossed two keys on the table and turned away, calling the dog. She poured herself tea, watched from the window as he went through the trees, Waldo bounding alongside, seizing and tossing twigs, tripping over his big paws, landing with a jolt to his jaw.

It was over, it was really over between them. Rowley had been so indifferent, not even pretending to be interested in what she said. One of them would soon have to do something about the divorce. Once she'd had so little to say to him, now there was so much she wanted to share and it was too late. Perhaps it always had been. Before he returned she left, leaving a note against the sugar bowl saying she'd gone to work.

It was a perfect spring day and she drove slowly, recalling childhood days with Beth, running over paddocks that had once spread so generously and now were over-built, the way they'd searched eagerly for the tiny orchids of spring, the dew cool on their bare feet. Damn! She was doing it again! Not concentrating on her driving. She pulled off the road because she'd been on the verge of an important discovery. What was it? Something about Beth, about love. Beth's death, complete in itself, yet the love she felt for Beth, still there, whole and perfect, with life of its own . . . a huge truck roared past but Ally was unaware of the way her car rocked in its slipstream; she was concentrating so hard, afraid of losing the thought, recognising its importance . . . the love you felt, did it exist, then, as something complete in itself? Ally's throat was aching, as though a huge lump was pressing against the skin.

Suddenly she decided to make a quick visit to Justina before she went to the refuge.

The lump in her throat slowly subsided. She kept her thoughts concentrated on the road.

Justina was down in the orchard and waved to her from among the elderly, gnarled trees.

'Come and see! Come and see, Ally, they're beginning to blossom.'

Ally noticed how low down the baby had moved. It seemed as though the birth wouldn't be long now. When she commented, Justina said, 'Gillie thought it might even be today, Ally. I'm to ring if I get any pains of any kind. You know we decided definitely, we'd have it here? I want my baby born right here, Ally. It's my first home. The first time I've ever felt I had a home.'

Justina had a strange little way of repeating facts, as though she was uncertain of them and wanted to make sure both you and she knew what she was saying. Ally put her arms around the girl, gave her a gentle hug.

'I understand, darling. And if Gillie and Viran agree, you haven't a worry in the world.'

'Oh, no, I haven't. I'm so lucky. It's so lucky you brought me up here, isn't it? Ally, I'd like you to be here when the baby gets born. Would you come?'

'I'm thrilled you've asked me. Of course I'll come.'

She felt nervous and elated at the same time. Her own experience of birth had been absolutely rotten. She wasn't at all sure she wanted to experience another woman's.

'Oh, Ally, you're just like a real mum to me. I really do feel you're like my own mum.'

Ally felt guilty for a moment. No paternalism, they said at the refuge and she always wanted to say, don't you mean maternalism? If Justina wanted to put her in the place her real mother couldn't or wouldn't fit into, where was the harm, especially in the big and scarey experience of giving birth?

When Ally got home late that afternoon, Waldo was chained on the back veranda and Rowley had gone. There was no note from him.

Viran phoned not long before midnight. It was time to go to Justina again.

Not wanting to have Waldo blundering around the small flat, she left him in the house and heard him howling as she drove away. The headlights washed the wattles by the track leading up to Gillie and Viran's mountain-top home. Inside, oil-lamps glowed with the same soft yellow of the wattle blooms.

Justina sat on the bed. Viran, short and chunky, was in his hospital whites. Gillie, as tall and slender as Viran was short and broad, sat by Justina, holding the girl's hand.

'It's coming along just fine, Ally. The head's engaged. Won't be long now.'

Viran had dark, curly hair, laughter lines around brown eyes, more lines around a wide-lipped mouth and, behind the imprint of laughter and good humour, emanated a steadfastness of purpose, some kind of dedication to humanity.

Gillie was different from Viran in every way, her height, her slenderness, so fine-boned, her blue eyes and her ruffled fair hair, yet she generated the same feeling of steadiness, reliability, concern for others.

They talked, listened to music, or sipped hot drinks. At times

Justina paced the room, once she went outside and walked as far as the orchard and back, at other times she lay on her side, groaning. For a while she slept and Ally dozed, too, a shout from Justina waking her. Ally looked dazedly around and focused on Viran's face.

She looked sleepily around the room, at its pieces of pottery, some chipped and crazed, macramé hangings Justina had made, flowers in old containers, a rug from St Vinnie's on the floor, a rocking chair Gillie had given her.

When Jane was born, Rowley had taken her to hospital at five in the morning. She was led away from him briskly, scarcely allowed time to say goodbye, looking anxiously over her shoulder as he walked away. It was cold and they made her sit down, in terrible discomfort from cramping pains. Questions and answers, the nurse filling in a form, herself saying, 'I don't care. I haven't got a religion, put anything you like.'

The girl had looked at her angrily, insisting, 'I have to put your religion down.' Ally, with a groan, said, 'Oh, all right. Presbyterian.' She remembered being taken off to a small room, a sister impersonally resting an ice-cold thing like a trumpet on her distended belly, listening for the baby's heartbeat, ignoring Ally's protest that the thing was cold. The horror of an enema being administered, no explanation as to what was being done or why, then the ignominy of being shaved around the pubic region; but above all the pain, the shivering from cold, wanting someone to be with her, someone she knew, someone who cared about her. Being left then in the labour ward, alone; glass-fronted cabinets with shining steel instruments.

From outside now came the dawn chorus of awakening birds and Gillie's reassuring voice, 'Here's the head, Jussie. Pant a little, girl, gently does it. Now a push, oh good, good.'

How different it had been for Ally. A nursing sister said crossly, 'I don't know why you mothers come in just as the shift's changing. Lie still now. I want you to take a good sniff of this, your doctor will be here soon. Come on, be a good girl, deep breaths please.' Something rubbery was clamped over her nose – she pushed it away frantically. She wasn't here for an operation! The sister said, 'It's for the baby's good! Don't you care about your baby? Your doctor's not here yet. Now breathe in, like a good girl.' Ally, defeated by the woman's superior knowledge and authority, breathed in and everything went hazy.

Justina's baby was emerging. Ally held her breath, deep emotion bringing tears to her eyes, a lumpiness to her throat. Justina had reached out to clutch her hand, groaning loudly as she pushed for the last time. The baby was flowing from her, smoothly and swiftly, now the head and the square little shoulders were out. Justina's groan had given way to a cry of ecstasy and joy. She had her arms held out, reaching for the little boy. Gillie moved the child quickly up on to her bare chest and Justina held him to her, tears flooding down her cheeks.

'Oh, he's perfect, isn't he? He's perfect, isn't he?'

'Yes, Justina, he's just beautiful and he's perfect.'

Justina sighed with relief. 'I was a bit scared, you know.'

'I know.'

Jane wasn't allowed to lie on her breast, nuzzling for her nipple. What a waste, what a cheating of them both. Jane, whisked away from her, not to be seen again for forty-eight long hours.

'She's premature! She needs special care. It's for the baby's good. You behave yourself.'

Ally was not allowed to get up, her breasts were hideously tight and painful, everything was such a mess. She endured the impersonal washing down of her genitals by a masked nurse, the pain of an injection into her buttocks.

'Why? What's wrong?'

'Your doctor ordered it. He knows what's best for you.'

Rowley was allowed to stay for only a few minutes, embarrassed by her hysterical demands that he make them bring the baby to her, telling her the baby was perfectly all right, he'd been allowed to see her in her little oxygen tent. The terror of not being told anything, the humiliation of being constantly treated like a backward child and then, on the third day when she'd staggered out of bed and gone stumbling down a corridor looking for the nursery, they'd rushed her back to bed in a hastily procured wheelchair and grudgingly brought Jane to her, put her into the mother's arms for three minutes exactly. Ally had gone very still and quiet, staring at the face of a complete stranger, with purplish lips, a tiny, pursed, disapproving mouth, turned down at the corners, the eyes firmly closed, wisps of fair hair on the fragile-looking scalp. She handed the baby back silently, and turned away as the nurse walked briskly off. By then she had been expressing milk to be fed by someone else from a bottle to Jane. She couldn't huddle on her side, face to the wall, as she felt like doing, for her breasts were still swollen and hurting. She didn't ask for the baby again and when they began routinely bringing Jane to her for feeding, she'd gritted her teeth against the agony when Jane at last began sucking weakly; she had felt indifferent, almost uncaring.

Now sunlight was pouring into the room. Viran had opened the door and the morning air was sweet with smells from the blossoms in the orchard.

Wrapped in a little rug, the boy slept in Justina's arms. Her eyes were closed, her breathing deep and even. Leaning over, Ally kissed her gently on the forehead, stayed staring into the little boy's face. The small, perfect lips were parted, the beautiful face completely relaxed.

Gillie and Viran, arm in arm, faces soft and contented, had gone to their own part of the big old house to get a few hours sleep before they went to work. Ally had said she wasn't in a hurry; she'd stay on until Gillie returned early in the evening.

Ally eased herself into an old-fashioned armchair, rested her head, closed her eyes, opening them now and then to look at the sleeping mother and child. Slowly, the pain and grief she'd been experiencing faded away and she felt her face take on the same softness and ease she'd perceived on Gillie's and Viran's. Nothing could ever alter the past. She could be glad that Justina, Jane, too, had a choice of how they wanted their baby to be born, of who they wanted around them when it happened.

Nine

For two days, the refuge house had been as though quaking in a miasma of contagious fear, the women constantly on the verge of hysteria. There'd been abusive phone calls, prowlers by night, footsteps on the path, blows on walls, tappings on windows.

Sylvia had sent Ally away early soon after lunch, saying, 'Just go somewhere and take it easy.'

Ally had turned her car on to the road that led to the hills and to Justina who'd become so dear to her, so uncomplex and loving in her response to friendship offered.

Justina had named her baby Virgil, an inspired combination and contraction of Viran and Gillie's names.

All afternoon, Ally helped Justina turn soil in the vegetable garden while Virgil slept in his basket. That morning Ally had taken Waldo to work with her and the women and children had made a fuss of him. After being shut in the house, he gambolled ecstatically around the orchard, tossing sticks, following scents, chasing a pair of aggressive, dive-bombing magpies. Ally had stayed to have dinner with Justina, while the exhausted dog sprawled on the veranda, body flat to the floorboards.

Viran and Gillie had come home and joined them. It was almost midnight when Ally drove up to her house. As she switched off, Waldo scrambled clumsily from the back seat over her lap and through the rolled-down window. Ally yelled after him. His claws were sharp. She left the car lights on while she switched on an overhead light and another that lit the back yard and the path leading to the house, a little uneasy because Waldo was now barking frantically. She turned off the car lights.

At the foot of the steps, Waldo leaped like a dancer. The back door lay within a small pool of shadow and within it something stirred.

Waldo dashed to her side and she grasped him by the collar.

'Who's there?'

Tall and bulky, he emerged from the darkness, carrying an axe with gleaming, honed-bright blade. He came slowly down the steps. She released Waldo and, yelping, the dog dodged behind her. Ally turned to run and tripped over Waldo. She rose on wounded knees to plead, 'No! Please, no!'

Waldo howled, tail curled under to protect belly and genitals. Ally scrambled upright and faced the man, looked into his face, smelled fumes of whisky, saw angry, mean eyes, and was possessed by terror. She felt her face twitching and her body shrinking in on itself. The axe that had been swinging low now lifted in the big hand. She ran again and, unbelievably, once more fell over Waldo who struggled violently and wrenched himself out from beneath her, yelping and howling. While she was still, nothing happened, so she stayed this time on hands and knees, trying to breathe quietly.

Then, without warning, came a blow on her back. Her legs and arms collapsed and she was flattened on the ground, screaming wildly. A second blow struck her on the back of the head and things shaped like bright fish danced in her vision. Her ears were roaring and she waited for the blood to fountain, shrinking in fearful anticipation of a third strike.

It didn't come. Dizzily, she groped, wondering why there was no blood. She rolled a little and saw Waldo, eyes deranged, body braced, jaws clamped on the arm of her attacker; heard, as the noise in her ears diminished, the dog's ferocious, muffled growling deep in his throat, the man's cries of pain as he shook his arm, trying to unlock the dog's jaws.

Brave Waldo, come into the fullness of his doghood, just in time to save her life.

Where were her keys? She had to get to the phone. How long could Waldo hang on to him?

Patting the grass distractedly, she crawled around, found the keys at last, stood and edged towards the house. She was walking in a strange, slanting way and abruptly the ground hit her in the face. Whimpering, she came up on an elbow.

'Get him off me.'

She was shocked, horrified. Nightmares aren't supposed to talk to you in high-pitched, whining voices, yet this one was, legs sprawled, one arm propping up his body, the other still in Waldo's growling grip, the axe behind them.

She stood up, crept around, darted in to pick it up, her head spinning as she bent, then she made her way to the garage where she took the key to a locked cupboard from a nail. She thrust the axe in the cupboard, burying the key afterwards in a box of rusting screws.

Feeling a little stronger, she went to the house, unlocked the door and at last called Waldo off. At once he released his victim and galloped to her, tail wagging wildly, laughing up at her. To her horror she saw blood on his big, white teeth.

'You've got to take me to a doctor.'

Jesus, he was talking to her again!

She shouted, 'I haven't got to do anything for you!'

Waldo growled and took a menacing, low-slung step towards the man.

'No, Waldo. Good boy. Stay, boy.'

Waldo sat, ears alert.

'I could have hit you with the blade. I could have chopped you to bits. I only wanted to frighten you; I didn't mean to hurt you real bad.'

Ally took a step forward, and said, 'All right. I'll phone someone. You'd better not move an inch while I'm doing it, though.'

Then, 'Who are you? Why did you do this? What's your name?'

'Lester Henriks.'

His voice was sullen. She nearly laughed out loud. Surely Lesters should be slim and graceful, not hulky-shouldered, big-faced and hairy?

Ally was no longer afraid of him. Suddenly she stamped down the steps and stood a few yards away from him, Waldo at her side.

'You'd better get up. There's a chair on the veranda. That grass is wet, you bloody fool.'

Without looking at her, he did as he was told. Quickly she walked back to the house, stood inside the screen door while he slumped into a chair, left Waldo guarding him while she tried to think, staring at the phone.

Viran. Of course, Viran. He'd know what to do. Viran listened to Ally's stumbling words and she heard a sharp intake of breath from him. He said he'd be there as fast as humanly possible, he'd come in an ambulance and she was to lock the door and stay inside. Instead, she walked back and stood watching the man.

'Why did you do that?' she asked him roughly. 'I've never seen you before in my life. How dare you come here and attack me. It was you, wasn't it, making a pest of yourself around the refuge, hanging around my house. You were down on the beach watching, weren't you?'

He answered, 'I don't have to tell you anything. Your dog's made a terrible mess of me arm. It's me right arm, too.'

'Well, naturally it's your right arm. That's the one you were holding the goddamned axe in, isn't it?'

Suddenly Ally thought of Fleur, goading and goading until a man hit her. Horrified, she shut the door and locked it, stood with her back against it, breathing fast. What was she doing? She was so angry, so furious over what had happened that she was in the grip of a desire to attack him physically. She'd never felt anything remotely like it before.

Well, it had happened, hadn't it? She'd been expecting something to happen to her. She'd known she couldn't go on navigating her way around other people's disasters without eventually colliding with one of her own.

She held her breath for a long moment. What if Fleur hadn't given the dog to her?

Waldo began to bark and she heard the sound of an engine approaching. She unlocked the door and went out. Nothing had ever looked so beautiful as the white ambulance pulling up at her back door, no one so splendid as Viran, hurrying to her. He passed what's-his-name, Lester, without a glance. Behind him, the driver walked up the steps, tipped his cap to her and stood over the man, gently taking his arm in one hand, looking closely at it, clucking his tongue.

Ally was trembling uncontrollably by the time she reached the hospital. A nurse came with a sedative. Viran came later to her private room, looked at her bruised back and sat gently stroking her forehead.

'Luckily, the skin is not broken, Ally. You will be stiff and sore for quite a while, though. The man's arm is bad. Very sharp teeth, your young dog has. I've given the man some shots. We'll see how he goes. He'll be with us for quite a while. That pup of yours will grow up into a dangerous animal, Ally, if you don't discipline him well.'

Ally said sleepily, 'Oh, Viran, you should have seen him. He was trying to hide behind me at first and I kept falling over him, then all of a sudden he knew what he had to do.'

'The blood of his fathers. They all have it, that breed.'

'*And* his mothers,' mumbled Ally. Viran's reply faded and she was asleep.

Some time in the night she woke briefly, heard someone walking swiftly down the passage, a distant rattling of metal on metal, thought of what had happened, of how close she'd come to being a headline in the newspapers. How furious Rowley would have been, wanting to shout at her, 'I told you so!' and not being able to, because she was all chopped up and dead, Jane left motherless.

In the morning, she ate the breakfast a smiling nurse brought, surprised at her hunger until she remembered working for hours in Justina's garden. Stiffly, she rolled out of bed and went to the shower. Viran met her in the passage on the way back to her room.

'Did I say you could get out of bed?'

'No, but I did and I'm all right. I'm going home.'

'If I say so you'll go home, Ally. Otherwise, not.'

Ally grinned to herself. Viran's command of the English language was very precise. He took her arm and led her back to her room, examined her back and her head.

'Not too bad. You'll wait until the doctor is here to examine you. I see what he says about going home.'

Lying down again, Ally didn't object too strenuously. She still felt shaken and a little nauseated.

'Will you phone the refuge, Viran. Tell them I won't be in today?'

He nodded.

'I phone the police, too. We'll get a policeman to the hospital to make your statement. I talked to them last night and they agreed.'

Ally stared at him, horrified.

'You phoned the police? I'm not going to lay any charges, Viran. No statement!'

Shocked, he looked at her. She went on, 'Viran, don't you see? I'm a refuge worker living in a lonely place. It'd get into the local paper and

I'd be the target for every nutcase on the peninsula.'

'Ally, I understand how you feel, but it's your duty . . .'

'You *don't* understand how I feel, Viran. You're a big, strong man . . .'

'I do understand the risk you take at the refuge. He is a violent man. His wife ran away and took their children. A neighbour told him she'd probably gone to the refuge.'

'He told you that? I knew it was because I worked there. He'd been harassing the refuge. It was him hanging around the house. He must have checked some of us out and decided I was the easiest to get at. I don't think his wife was even in our refuge. If she had any sense she's further away than Parktown.'

'And so you just want me to take you home and then later he can walk out of my hospital any time he pleases?'

'Yes. That's right.'

Viran sighed.

'All right, Ally. I can't force you, nor can the police. If that's what you want.'

'That's what I want. Whatever I do, I'm going to be scared stiff now, any time I hear a sound outside, every time Waldo barks. He's ruined my sense of security.'

'I know, Ally. I'm not angry. I understand.'

After lunch, Ally was driven home in the ambulance, sitting beside the driver, wincing when her back touched the seat.

She made sure the house was locked up before she went to rest. In the evening, she went outside to feed Waldo. The garage door was open and suddenly she remembered the axe, locked away in a cupboard. He'd come back for that, some time. He'd come back. Not right away, but some time he'd be back. What if he had a gun next time? What if he shot Waldo first? What if he'd had a gun instead of an axe last night? Which refuge would he target next, who'd be his next victim? If he found his wife, what would he do to her?

Ally went inside, dressed herself, then went out and unlocked the cupboard, got the axe and put it on the back seat of the car, called Waldo, then drove off to the police station.

117

Ten

One Sunday, Lynsey came to lunch. The weather was warming up at last. They walked slowly along the beach, sat among leaning banksia trees, birds busy stabbing with strong beaks at the stiff, pale lemon, bottle-brush flowers. They ate a vegetable quiche Lynsey had brought with her and opened a dry Riesling from the Hunter valley.

In the early evening, they looked westward to a flamboyant sunset. An atmospheric freakiness sent spears of pale green and orange, streaked vividly with scarlet, into a darkening arch, as though from an alien sun.

'Did you ever see an aurora, Ally?'

'Pardon?'

'An aurora Australis. Funny, why don't we get them any more? I remember seeing two, maybe three, when I was little.'

Ally, watching the sky, was silent, then a memory stirred of some majestic, nocturnal display, rippling waves of mauve, pink, rose, blue, green, deepening dramatically, fading delicately, herself watching from the warmth of her father's arms.

'Yes, I saw one. I'd completely forgotten.'

How could she have forgotten that? It had been her tenth birthday. How could she possibly have forgotten the feeling of snuggling against her father's solid chest, of the strength of those big arms holding her securely, of his voice saying, 'Hey, birthday girl, take a good look at your special aurora. You mightn't ever see one again. They don't get turned on for just anybody, you know.'

It was *after* Beth had died and he'd held her close, spoken lovingly, tenderly.

After Lynsey had gone, she kept thinking about the night of the aurora. Were there other memories of love that she'd blanked from her mind? Was forgetting the good memories, part of the punishment? Was it she who'd done the punishing, not her father?

She and Beth, that morning, after weeks of rain. The two of them running down the long, sloping paddock, the musky smell of capeweed, the sweetness of jonquils, tiny, yellow flower cups nodding delicately in the wind of their passing. Picking the flowers, pollen dusting their fingers. Ally sat slitting the stems, green sap collecting under her thumbnail, the daisy chains stretching away from her, yard after yard, she so absorbed in making them, with the sun warm on her shoulders, and Beth wandering away, picking more flowers.

Suddenly Beth had screamed.

Over and over, she'd been told never to take Beth close to the creek, never, not even when it was a harmless trickle. That day, after the rain, it was a raging torrent and Beth had wandered close, perhaps to throw sticks. Part of the bank caved in. Ally remembered the fresh earth in the deep crack where the chunk of bank had slipped and Beth, struggling, screaming, was swept away.

Shivering, Ally rubbed her arms, her body cold, all these years after, her breath coming unevenly.

Her screams had brought her mother flying down the paddock. There was nothing to be done, for Beth had disappeared. Her mother had plunged in, floundered about, Ally shrieking, believing her mother would vanish beneath the surface as Beth had done.

Her father had been brought home by a policeman. He must have been, for there was a policeman in the background somewhere. Her mother had collapsed after dragging herself from the creek, carried to the house by neighbours, who'd gone back and kept searching.

And afterwards, after they'd found the child's body downstream, he'd stood over her, her father, arms raised, shouting in a terrible voice like the roar of an angry god, 'You were told. You were told. I told you, never take Beth near the creek', and she was hurried out of the room by someone, in her ears the awful sound of her father sobbing, a vision of his great height crumpling to the floor. No tears from her. No tears at all; she wept only in her dreams, those groaning, sobbing dreams that had so disturbed Rowley and woken Jane.

No wonder Jane had fled from Max. How could he unravel her nightmares, when poor Jane was only echoing those of her selfish, stupid mother?

Slowly Ally rose, put milk into a saucepan, her hands moving jerkily. For nearly half a century she'd hidden, camouflaged, fled from memories of that day and yet she intimately knew each moment of it, the smell of flowers, the feel of gentle wind, sounds of the rushing creek, the contentment she'd felt listening to her small sister's happy voice, the last contentment she'd felt in her life.

Her thoughts were moving so sluggishly, trying to slide away. Memories remained in her mind, the record of tragedy, seen through . . . the milk bubbled suddenly to the rim of the saucepan and she whipped it from the heat, poured it into a mug, sat holding it in both palms.

Something was trying to elude her. Some thought. Something terribly important. What had she been thinking when the milk nearly boiled over?

Seen through the eyes . . . that day, seen through the eyes, her eyes, the eyes of an eight-year-old child, frightened, grief-stricken, guilty.

She set the milk down on the table. Not the recorded memory of a mature and compassionate woman. That is what I have become, she thought, a mature and compassionate woman, who sees that her father would not for a moment have remembered that cry of blame, would have been horrified if he'd known what he'd said and how it had affected the frail psyche of his surviving child. Whom he had loved.

Whom he had loved! Of course he'd loved her! Of course he hadn't blamed her, except for that one fleeting moment.

All those years of not understanding, of never permitting herself to re-examine, reassess. All those years assuming an eight-year-old child had accurately interpreted the emotions of a distraught father. Punishing herself, as no one else wanted to punish her, for no one but she had thought she should be punished.

Some time over the past year she'd healed herself of the sad delusion that she was responsible for the death of her little sister. How long was it since she'd had one of the dreams? They had been dreams of being rooted to a spot, unable to reach Rowley, Jane, Fleur, whoever was featuring that night in her dream, voiceless, trying to scream for help; dreams of floods, tidal waves, of the ocean engulfing the house. Healed, and she hadn't noticed. Some time over the past year, she had begun to grow outward instead of inward.

Ally finished drinking the now cool milk. She felt incredibly tired. That night she dreamed her mind had become a glittering cave; thoughts like crystal columns touched and rang with an echo of amazing beauty. Disembodied faces drifted by, Ben among them. She was a young girl, running to meet Ben, but as fast as she ran his face receded and then Jane glided swiftly past her, laughing. Ben's face merged into Jane's. From far away, a rapidly moving figure became Fleur, and Ally cried out in her sleep, for Fleur's face was worn and bruised, lined and bleeding.

A violent sound splintered the cave and pieces flew sparkling in all directions. Waldo was barking hysterically and she woke to the shattering disturbance of a low-flying jet.

Ally lurched from her bed, bumping dazedly into the door-frame. Waldo followed her to the kitchen, crashed to the floor, head on paws, looking up at her with eyes showing a line of white beneath the iris. She whipped an egg into skimmed milk for him.

Fleur's face was still vividly in her mind. She went to the phone, sighed with relief when her friend answered.

'Hey, I've got the day off, Fleur. Going to be a gorgeous day. Why don't we play tennis?'

That weekend, Ally began a project she'd often thought of; she was making the garden over into a bush garden, getting rid of everything but native coastal plants and trees. It was a ridiculous time of the year to begin with, the earth hard and the heat growing.

Fleur helped in desultory fashion for a while, then lay on a rug in the shade of a tree, watching Ally and brushing tiny black bush flies from her face.

'Oh, Ally, it's too hot to work like that. Aren't the bloody flies driving you crazy? Let's go for a swim. You're making me feel guilty.'

Ally threw down her trowel, only too ready to be persuaded away from what she was doing.

The surf was perfect that day, waves breaking in waist-deep water where they were easy to catch, enough power within them to carry the surfers right up on to the sand.

At first they called to each other as they waded laboriously out again for the next wave, diving beneath those that had already broken or weren't quite ready. Soon they were silent, each intent on the challenge of inserting her stretched body at the precise point where it would become part of the wave, arms held rigid, slightly beneath the body, shoulders a little hunched, legs stretched and curved upwards. Riding the crest, they became helpless, hearts pounding in anticipation of the moment when the foaming curl would collapse, precipitating them down the face of the breaker, where the slightest miscalculation would plunge them to the bottom, there to be pounded and rolled and swung without mercy. Perfection was to stay with the shape, dropping from its height to its lowest point and continuing to sweep shoreward until the wave died.

Ally loved the sound of an approaching wave, that pause in the roaring when the wave rose intact, its mighty shoulders solid, the wall of it growing thinner at the top, finer, until there began a faint susurration, a trembling that collapsed into the finest of frothing fingers tickling its length, a curling over, while her heart pounded in fear and excitement and she made the decision to take it or to dive quickly beneath.

Only when they were staggering from exhaustion did they leave the surf, red-eyed and tangle-haired, squinting in the brightness of the high noon sun.

After they'd showered, Ally took cold beer on to the shaded veranda and they drank contentedly.

Fleur said casually, 'Ally, what do you do about sex, now Rowley's gone?'

Ally gripped the light aluminium beer can so hard that beer squirted, splashing her cheeks. She wiped it away with the palm of her hand. Fleur stared, then began to laugh.

'Jesus, Ally, you really are something. I embarrassed you, didn't I? You've been working at a women's refuge for months! So how can a simple question like that make you go ga-ga? Don't answer me. Sorry I opened my big mouth. Keep it a secret, love. I suppose that's why you work so hard in the garden, huh? Duckie, there are things you can do, you know.'

Ally said, 'Did it ever occur to you that some people might prefer to be celibate?'

'Oh, pardon me, Allys June. Change of subject. There's a Beethoven programme on at the town hall next week, feel like coming with me?'

'Yes, love to. Hang on, Fleur. I know I went on like a prude. You know what, I've started to go a bit queer around men lately. I was at a meeting the other day and there was this one guy there, a welfare worker, and suddenly I started wondering what it'd be like to be in bed with him. I had the ghastly feeling he picked up on what I was thinking, because he began to shift around, crossing and re-crossing his legs.'

Fleur grinned.

'You'd have no trouble getting a bloke, you know. Your figure's terrific and you look ten years younger than your age. What do you do about sex, Ally? I'm curious.'

'I don't do anything. Look, I'm not an idiot, I've been to a sexuality workshop and I can say fuck without stuttering and I know there are lots of things you can do for yourself . . .'

'Well, Ally, I've tried everything. Doing things to yourself is lonely. Jesus, it's lonely. Effective in a tension-releasing way, but I always feel like howling with loneliness after. And I'm scared that if I get too good at doing things to myself with vibrators and stuff, blokes won't be able to satisfy me.' She laughed. 'I nearly drowned myself when I had my spa bath installed, trying to position myself the right distance from one of the jets to get a buzz out of it. Darned thing was too powerful. I finished up all numb.'

'I wish you hadn't started this conversation, Fleur. I'm starting to worry about sex. How on earth am I going to meet somebody suitable?'

'Not at the refuge, that's for sure, Ally. Hey, what about that spunky bloke, the one that's a matron or something, what's-his-name.'

'Viran? He lives with Gillie, you donkey. Anyway, he's twenty years younger than me.'

'So? That's nothing. Women our age are much sought after by younger men, didn't you know? We don't hassle them, we're grateful, we don't get pregnant on them.'

Fleur went on with a wicked grin, 'Just make sure you don't start anything with a very young one, they're much too energetic, wear you out.'

Ally leapt to her feet.

'Well, I'm starving. I'm going to make something for lunch.'

Ally kept working in her garden. She drove for miles to plant nurseries, looking for things that would thrive in salty air. Her body grew leaner and more tanned, her nose peeled.

The weather changed abruptly. Cold winds swept up from the Antarctic. The gigantic swirl of a vast depression slipped towards Tasmania from far up in the tropics where it had begun, bringing great waves crashing ponderously to the shore. From far out they came, each small mountain of water approaching the land in tall, quaking walls, until the final topple, booming with a last, far-reaching surge of energy that brought the ocean, spent and foaming to her feet.

Ally, sitting on a rock that had a smooth part like a saddle into which her bottom fitted, watched the majestic panorama before her. How lucky she was to live so close to that ever-changing drama. She'd like to have surfed, but it would have been suicidal to enter that maelstrom.

There was a strange little nagging feeling she had. After a while, she recognised it. She was feeling lonely. She wanted someone to share the day with her. Once she'd have leapt to her feet, run away from the feeling. Perhaps later she could go and visit Jane. With a feeling of guilt, she realised she hadn't phoned Jane or been to see her in weeks. Why hadn't Jane been in touch? She should go and see her right away.

But Ally stayed on the beach. All right, she didn't want to go and see Jane. She had been thinking about so many things lately, none of them to do with Jane, her daughter. Ally shuffled around on her rock. She was going to have to come to terms with it sooner or later. It wasn't going to go away. In two or three months the baby would be born.

Perhaps it was time she began thinking about moving on from the refuge. The burn-out signs were starting to appear, the slight inner flinching when a distraught woman approached, the myopic conviction growing that the world was full of violent men and unhappy women, when she knew that in reality it was not, the paranoia about always locking doors and windows, anticipating that another Lester, or Lester himself, would be waiting for her when she came home late at night. The constant presence of Waldo gave her a feeling of security. Without him, Ally knew she'd have been too afraid to continue living at the beach house. Perhaps she should think about having it converted into two separate units. It could be done quite easily and the rent she received would eventually cover the cost.

What a messy year it had been. She was to see Walt next week about a divorce. Rowley had gone overseas again, Walt had told her in passing. Strange not to know what he was doing.

Funny, a year ago she'd had no problems at all, had been unaware of Fleur's problems, unsure of Jane's or Rowley's. Now everywhere she looked there were problems, things to be done because of commitments made. What was going to happen to Fleur as she grew older? Herself, if it came to that?

And Justina, she'd been avoiding thinking about that. Ally got up and paced restlessly, then returned to her rock. Yesterday Gillie had called in at the refuge to see her. Justina and Virgil had gone. Hugh had somehow tracked her down, turned up driving in an old Holden and within an hour the girl had packed and gone off with him. She'd left no message for Ally but had gone off with the gaunt man with sunken eyes and shaking body, leaving Gillie helplessly waving from the veranda. Ally pressed a hand to her chest, alarmed. A thin pain, like a stabbing blade, was attacking her in the region of her heart. She sat very still, afraid to move.

After a few minutes the pain went away. Ally stood up slowly and began cautiously to walk back towards the house. Abruptly she remembered Sylvia on the first day she'd gone to the refuge – how long ago it seemed now – telling her about the kind of work she'd be doing, and she'd said something, in passing, about a pain near the heart. A pain as though something was sticking into her heart and

Sylvia had said how afraid she'd been until she realised she felt it only when she was listening to what some woman had endured, not when she was dashing around doing things; a pain that developed with the job.

Ally felt relieved. The pain had come when she thought of Justina and that beautiful child gone from the safety and serenity of the house on the hillside, and, right on cue, the pain came again. She'd made the mistake of allowing Justina to come into her life, had become much too close to her. That's why maternalism/paternalism was so frowned on within the refuge system, of course. Not just because it was weakening for those in need of support, but because it could become devastating for the refuge worker, too.

Ally climbed the back steps, feeling tired and sad. Perhaps she'd hear from Justina one day, perhaps she'd never hear from her again.

Eleven

Ally and Viran stood on the footpath outside Pinky's in Parktown, where they'd lunched after Lester Henriks's appearance before the magistrate.

Ally said bitterly, 'He scrubbed up well, didn't he?'

Viran nodded. 'Yes, the court didn't see the man you and I saw that night, Ally. Bed rest and good food made a big change in him, talking to the psychiatrist, too, that helped him a lot. I know you don't like shrinks, Ally, but some of them are very excellent.'

Ally smiled, 'Jane used to call them spychrists. The magistrate made it sound as though I had no right to keep a dog to protect me.'

'It was the scar on Lester's arm that made him angry, I think. That made a very good defence for Lester.'

'What's going to happen to him now, Viran. What will he do, do you think?'

Viran said thoughtfully, 'I think he'll be very careful, Ally, afraid that next time he does the violent thing, he will go to gaol. It was made clear to him. I thought you were a good witness.'

'Do you know what I think? I think he'll go underground. People do. You never change them.' She paused and stared at Viran. 'Do you really mean that – I was a good witness?'

Viran glanced at her as they strolled along the street. He took her arm.

'Let's sit in the sun for a while, Ally, over there, where we can look on the sea.'

Sitting on the bench, he went on: 'What do you mean by underground?'

'Oh, I just mean, he'll keep right on looking for his wife and kids and it's possible that when he finds them he'll make sure next time nobody lives to get him into trouble with the law.'

'My God, Ally, I hope you are not right. You are being very negative. Perhaps it is time you thought about not working at the refuge. It is a very negative place.'

Ally sighed.

'I know that. I think maybe you're right.'

'Gillie was talking about it to me. She thought you were looking tired. There are other jobs, Ally, now that you have the refuge experience up your arm . . .'

'Sleeve, Viran. Up your sleeve.' Ally smiled at her friend. 'Yes, I guess that's right. I do have experience now, don't I? Anyway, I can't help feeling mad as hell that Henriks got off with a fine and a good behaviour bond. It makes me sick. The legal system seems to be prejudiced on the man's side.'

'I certainly received the feeling that the gentleman on the bench wouldn't allow *his* wife to be working at a women's refuge.'

Ally grinned. 'He looked just the way Rowley, my hus . . . my ex-husband, looked when he found out I was working there.'

'It's good your name won't be printed in the newspaper. That's good, eh?' Viran stood up and sighed, 'Ah, this sun is so good, but I must go back to the hospital.'

Ally watched him go. What would it be like to get into bed with Viran? She shivered, then stood quickly and walked through the ti-tree windbreak to the well-trodden Parktown beach. The bay was so quiet and flat after the ocean.

She *was* feeling tired. Time she thought about new directions, time to have a break. She'd see more of Fleur, go to see Jane – and Marjorie. She had to begin trying harder to understand, to value, their lives.

Their lives were unconventional, they needed her support. Nothing she said or did was going to change one thing about her daughter's life. It would be a waste of energy, as well as a betrayal of the relationship they were slowly building up.

It occurred to her then that, somewhere in the past year, she'd learned to step back a little, to evaluate problems, to decide whether they were hers or not hers. She saw this to be a valuable change. By disentangling herself from the emotion of someone's problem, she was able to see more clearly the pattern of their direction, to react to it less fearfully.

Suddenly, Ally's mind was made up. She began to walk briskly back to her car. When she got to the refuge, Sylvia was alone in the office and it was a good time to talk to her.

Sylvia, listened, said, 'Ally, there's several months' solid experience behind you now. I agree. It's the right time for you to have a break. Here, I put this out for you, as it happens. It's a new course at the college of advanced education.'

Ally read the brochure.

'It sounds like a good course. I'd love to do it.'

'Well, why not? It'd give you that little bit of theory that you need to go with your practical work and it's only a nine-month commitment.'

Ally said doubtfully, 'You don't think I'm too old?'

'No, you're not too old. What are you going to do with yourself if you don't keep on working?'

Ally put the paper down. 'Absolutely nothing and that would probably be disastrous. Can I take this?'

'Sure. Ally, I don't know if I'm supposed to know this. I saw Marjorie this afternoon. She told me about Jane and the baby. I feel so happy for you.'

Ally swallowed nervously.

'Sylvia, do you know the situation between Jane and Marjorie?'

'Living together? Yes, of course.'

'I mean . . . well, *really* living together. In a lesbian relationship.'

Sylvia said gently, 'You having a bit of trouble with that one, Ally?'

Ally nodded, then smiled, 'I'm making progress, I think.'

'Ally, do you know Marjorie well?'

'I've known her for a long time, but I don't think I know her at all.'

'She's incredibly highly respected, you know, not just in the women's movement, but professionally and politically. Regarded as having great integrity and honesty. I admire her very much.'

127

Funny, she thought, that's just what people used to say about Verna.

Ally said slowly, 'And you think that should make it easier for me to accept the way things are with her and my daughter? You admire her and I accept that, but to me she's a woman who's destroyed my daughter's life, possibly my grandchild's life, too.'

Sylvia said gently, 'Your daughter's life or the hopes you laid on her, Ally?'

Ally remained silent for a while. Sylvia said nothing. It occurred to Ally how comfortable that silence was. Once she would have jumped up and fled from it.

'I understand what you're saying, what you're reminding me of. I can't expect her to live her life by my rules. Yes, I can accept that. I can learn to live with it. What about the baby, Sylvia, it's not her choice, his choice. Isn't this something Jane is laying on her baby?'

'No more than anyone lays on a child when they make the decision to have one, or have one without making any decisions. You have no control over that either, have you? The child will have to handle that, make decisions. If you choose, you can be there, a supportive grandparent.'

'If I choose now to be a supportive mother?'

Sylvia nodded. 'Times are changing, Ally. Everyone has many more choices now.'

The phone rang and Sylvia answered it. Ally watched her face, saw the two little lines appear between her eyebrows, noted the way Sylvia's body slumped in the chair a little, heard the agitated voice from the other end of the line.

She moved closer to Sylvia, put her arms around her and, for a moment, rested her cheek against the other woman's soft hair. Sylvia's free arm came up to return the hug.

On the way home, Ally thought of what Sylvia had said. There really was nothing she could do but accept that Jane had made certain decisions that her mother would not have wanted her to make, yet they were a fact of their lives now and it had been Jane's right to make them. She remembered the day she and Jane had first talked freely to each other, how they'd impulsively linked arms and the way the contact of skin had made both of them flinch, so that the simple intimacy of that moment had quickly ended.

Justina's baby had been given to her at once, the tiny boy seeming almost to sink into his mother's flesh, as though renewing the bonding of the months when he'd floated within her womb. She'd seen then so clearly how the immediate coming together again of mother and child after birth had been a renewal of that pre-birth oneness, and it was something she and Jane had never experienced. Ally felt sharp pain, a moment of intense and hopeless grief, for there was no way that early damage could be repaired now.

Her spirits lifted. She had the baby to look forward to, months in which she could talk to Jane. Jane, of course, would know all about bonding and its importance for the later development between mother and child, but she could reinforce it anyway, to make sure Jane wouldn't allow the same mistake to happen to her.

Ally decided that next day she'd go shopping for a few things for the baby. There were beautiful baby clothes available. It would be such a lot of fun having a look at them, deciding what to get.

At home she went to the phone at once and dialled Jane's number. Marjorie answered, sounding very animated.

'Ally! We were just talking about you. I'll put Jane on.'

Jane's voice held the same excitement.

'Hi Mum! You must have e.s.p. I was about to phone you.'

'Jane, I wondered if you and Marjorie would come to dinner. I suppose tonight's too short notice?'

'What about tomorrow, Mum? We're going out tonight. We're celebrating. Something absolutely incredible's happened. Marjorie's got a study grant to go to the UK for a year. It could even be two years. We're so excited. It's marvellous for her.'

Ally's heart seemed to give a little leap. Marjorie was going away. Thousands of miles away, would be away when the baby came, perhaps for many months afterwards. The baby's birth would change Jane in ways she couldn't begin to understand at this stage. For a moment she thought of Ben.

'A study grant? How wonderful, Jane.'

'Isn't it? We'd almost forgotten she'd applied for it. Didn't think she had a hope of getting it.'

'That's really tremendous. Please congratulate her for me.'

'OK. We'll come over about five tomorrow afternoon, Mum. We're leaving at the end of next week. Marjorie has to take the grant up in six weeks, so we're off to America to stay with her mother and stepfather for a week or so, then we'll fly to London. I can't believe it's happening.'

Jane. Jane going too. Jane would be on the other side of the world when the baby was born. She wouldn't be shopping for the baby, or, if she was, she'd be sending parcels to England.

Jane was saying, 'It'll be terrific to see Dad again. You knew he was over there, Mum?'

'Yes.' Her voice was faint. Ally cleared her throat.

Jane said, 'We'll be staying with Dad until we get a place of our own. He's renting a house not too far out of London and it sounds gorgeous, really old and quaint.'

'He's been writing to you, Jane?'

'Oh yes, Dad always stays in touch. He's good like that. Mum, you knew he'd met someone over there? Sounds really serious this time. She seems rather nice. I've spoken to her on the phone.'

Ally stared down at her hand. Without realising it, she'd picked up a ballpoint pen and there was an ugly scratch etched deep into the polished wood of the phone table. She was still dragging the pen across the surface, leaning down on it with all her strength. Something like bile had filled her throat. She swallowed and there was a sharp, bitter taste. Her thoughts had become utterly confused. She felt disoriented. She felt angry, massively angry, her chest full of an unpleasant thudding. She mustn't let Jane hear how she was feeling.

Jane was saying, 'Hey, Mum, are you still there? I didn't upset you, did I?'

Ally said brightly, 'No, of course not, darling, that all sounds really exciting all round. Listen, I have to go, I've got something on the stove. See you tomorrow.'

Suddenly, everything had fallen apart again. She was the outsider, the watcher on the lonely shore, observing others drifting away from her.

Jane would be sharing her pregnancy with Rowley and his new woman, his new 'lady'. Who sounded rather nice. Not too weak, like Ally. Not too strong, like Verna. Just right for Rowley.

They'd be having wonderful experiences, lots of fun and stimulation. She'd wanted so much to enter a time of closeness and understanding with Jane, to be the caring, sensitive, supportive parent Jane had never known. Jane had learned only too well to live without Ally's support or love. The importance she'd thought to have begun assuming in Jane's life, was a reflection of her own need.

The bitterness rose again in her throat.

Why hadn't she given Jane an honest reaction to her news, let her hear her disappointment, shock, surprise, anything but that false, phoney voice she'd used.

Like a small whirlwind, a new crisis had boiled up to engulf her and within it she sensed danger; depression and despair loomed.

She was frightened.

Was it possible that the changes she'd so painfully made in her life could evaporate, plunging her back into the black hole?

Ally jumped up, reached for the car keys, left Waldo sprawled on the veranda, head on paws, while she drove away.

She went to the refuge. As she unlocked the door, a bedraggled figure rushed to hug her. Winnie was back again, looking a little tidier, more together.

'I'm so glad to see you Ally.'

Winnie clutched her arm, walked into the office with her.

'Ally, I was too off my head to talk to you much before, but you know, I never forgot that first day you was here. You had a fuckwit like me to handle and you done it so gentle and kind. I just found out, you've been bashed up, just like a lot of us.'

'I wasn't hurt much, Winnie. And you're not a fuckwit . . .'

'Jeez, if I could get my hands on the bloke that done that to you, Ally, I'd carve him up. You should've let me go for him that day, remember, the day you took the knife away from me?'

'I remember. But it wasn't the same man.'

'Doesn't matter. I'd have got one of them, wouldn't I? You staying? I'll make you a cup of coffee.'

Winnie padded away to the kitchen. Ally could hear voices from all over the house but the office was empty. She sat in the big chair. It was amazing how deeply so many women had reacted when they heard of the way she'd been attacked. She hadn't given it much thought until now, when she saw how emotionally involved Winnie felt. When Fleur heard about it, she'd come rushing to Ally, sobbing, saying, 'I ask for it, Ally, but you don't. The rotten swine could have killed you. Thank God you had Waldo. It must have been our guardian angels made me get him for you.'

Jane had heard from Sylvia, had come to see her mother, alarmed and upset, wanting Ally to sell the house and move somewhere closer in. Marjorie had rung, talked to her gravely, made no suggestions, crediting her with accepting the risks of the kind of work she was involved in.

Thinking of Winnie, hearing her rattling around in the kitchen, Ally had a sudden realisation of how the women who came into the refuge had enriched her life, enriched it beyond logical assessment. Despairing, grieving, schizophrenic, disturbed, struggling to break free of legal and illegal drugs, dragging children with them, or childless, laughing, cursing, crying, shouting, whispering, they came not only seeking refuge, but in hope of change and a better life.

She leaned her head back, closed her eyes. The day she entered this house, she'd become part of a community, a woman of value, as they all were.

She'd been so nervous and afraid that first day. How thankful she was that she'd gone back and kept going back until she was part of it.

Winnie came in with two mugs of coffee and settled herself on the floor at Ally's feet.

'Winnie, when you get depressed, what do you do?'

'What do you mean, what do I do?'

'I mean . . . what do you do about the feeling? Does it frighten you? Are you scared you won't come out of it?'

'No! I always come out of it. You saw me that day, didn't you? Don't you remember? I went to sleep. It's a fuckin' nuisance, getting attacks of being depressed, but I know I'll come out of it. I always do. Everyone does, don't they?'

The coffee was horrible, but Ally sipped it, scarcely noticing.

'You mean, you're kind of patient about it?'

'Yes. I had to learn that. I mean, if you don't, you're dead, aren't you?' Winnie grinned. 'Hey, I'm counselling you, aren't I?'

'You sure are, Winnie. Thank you. That sorted something out for me.'

She smiled at the woman. What was it Sylvia had said once? They were all in it together, everyone had problems of one kind or another.

'Well, thanks for the coffee and the talk, Winnie. I only came in for a minute. I have to go and see my daughter.'

Winnie said wistfully, 'That's nice, having a daughter. Is she married?'

'She's having a baby,' said Ally. She hesitated for a moment and then went on, 'but she's not married.'

'You'll be a grandma. Oh, that's lovely, Ally. I wish I'd had children.'

Ally stood up.

'She's going overseas, Winnie. Very soon. She'll be a long way from me when the baby's born. She'll be in England.'

'Oh, that's a shame. England – they have women's refuges over there. I read about them. I think that's where they started them, isn't it? Why don't you save up the air fare, it's not all that much, and go and work in a refuge in England, Ally? Then you'll be there when the baby's born. Your daughter'll need you around, won't she, if she's not married?'

Ally stared blankly at Winnie.

'Winnie, you're fantastic!'

Winnie said modestly, 'I know. When I'm not nuts, I can get pretty smart. You got any other problems, Ally?'

'No, not a one, Winnie. I'm going now. See you later, and Winnie, thanks a lot for your help.'

She had the most extraordinary feeling of excitement.

Ally was only a little way down the street when the tail-end of the conversation with Winnie replayed itself in her mind. Misleading. Dishonest. Saying Jane wasn't married, letting Winnie think she'd need her mother around for support, seeing herself in that role. Phoney again.

She groaned, hit the steering wheel with her fist, slammed on the brakes and did a U-turn. Rushing up the path to the security door again, she called, 'Winnie, where are you, Winnie?'

As she unlocked the door and walked in, Winnie appeared in the foyer, looking startled.

'I just wanted to tell you, Winnie, my daughter, you know, I was telling you she's having a baby?'

Winnie nodded.

'I said she wasn't married but that was misleading. She doesn't really need me around at all, not for support anyway, because she's . . . she's in a lesbian . . . relationship with a marvellous woman. But I'm thinking about going over anyway. That was a great idea of yours. Thanks, Winnie. Goodbye again.'

Winnie stood motionless as Ally swung away to open the door, then she called, 'Hang on, Ally! Did you come all the way back just to tell me that?'

Ally turned and nodded, 'I thought it was important.'

Winnie burst out laughing.

'Gee, Ally, if you do go away, we'll miss you! Drive carefully now.'

JOAN RILEY
The Unbelonging

Summoned to Britain by a father she has never known, eleven-year-old Hyacinth exchanges the warmth and exuberance of the backstreets of Jamaica for the gloom of inner-city London. She finds herself in a land of strangers, the only black face in a sea of white.

Faced at school with the hostility of her classmates, and at home with violence from her father and a threatening sexuality she does not understand, she seeks refuge in dreams of her homeland – dreams which she must eventually test against the truth.

In her first book black novelist Joan Riley paints a vivid portrait of immigrant experience in Britain, refusing to compromise by romanticising its harsh reality.

Fiction　　　　　　0 7043 3959 5　　　　　　£3.95

JOAN BARFOOT
Duet for Three

Aggie is eighty, and dying. Helpless, unwiedly, incontinent, her body is slipping out of control, and she can only remember the heady independence of those happy years after the death of her husband. Now she is dependent on her ageing daughter June, a woman who can neither accept nor offer love. Her consolation is the passionate love she feels for her granddaughter Frances, a free spirit whose dreams and desires, this time, will perhaps not be destroyed by the forces of circumstance and convention.

Joan Barfoot is the author of two much loved previous novels *Gaining Ground* and *Dancing in the Dark* – both of which are still in print with The Women's Press.

| *Fiction* | 0 7043 3981 1 | £3.95 |
| *Hardcover* | 0 7043 2872 0 | £8.95 |

SHIZUKO GŌ
Requiem

'I must fulfil the responsibility of a survivor, on behalf of the dead who cannot speak for themselves; I must say what should be done' *Shizuko Gō*

The year is 1945. Setsuko is 16 years old, Naomi is 14. Amid sickness, starvation and death, the two girls find comfort in friendship. They argue about patriotism, honour, democracy.

Then comes the bombing of Yokohama. It is saturation bombing, firebombing. It brings destruction beyond imagining, and the end of their world.

Shizuko Gō was herself 16 in 1945, and she survived the bombing of Yokohama. She waited nearly 30 years to write this immensely moving and powerful novel, which won the Akutagawa Prize, Japan's premier literary award, in 1973.

| *Fiction* | 0 7043 3961 7 | £2.95 |
| *Hardcover* | 0 7043 2863 1 | £7.95 |

JAN CLAUSEN
Sinking, Stealing

Josie and Ericka are runaways on a Greyhound bus trip across America, using assumed names and forged documents. Theirs is no ordinary relationship, for Ericka is ten years old, and Josie is not her mother, though she has been a parent to her for most of her life. Rhea, Ericka's mother and Josie's lover, has been killed in a recent accident and Ericka's father has gained legal custody.

Josie and Ericka struggle to maintain a parent-child relationship in the face of relentless opposition from an angry father and a society that does not recognise any legal or social bond between them. Their relationship is not an easy one – they each must cope with the loss of Rhea and face the possibility that their attachment to one another will not be allowed to survive.

The adventures on the journey are sometimes harrowing and sometimes funny, but always observed with a wry and affectionate wit. Jan Clausen, well known for her poetry and stories, writes here with enormous skill, sensitivity and integrity.

Fiction 0 7043 3953 6 £3.95